The
Property Investment
Playbook

Also by the authors

Essential Property Investment Calculations
Robert Heaton

The Property Investment Playbook – Volume 1
Robert Heaton & Ye Feng

The Property Investment Playbook – Volume 2
Robert Heaton & Ye Feng

The
Property Investment
Playbook

Volume 1

*A complete course in property investment,
buy-to-let investing and property development*

Robert Heaton & Ye Feng

Get the free resources

I've prepared some free materials to accompany the book. All you need to do to access them is head over to my website. These materials include the following:

- a "dreamlining" spreadsheet to help you set your property goals
- a spreadsheet for assessing basic buy-to-let property deals
- a spreadsheet for modelling property refurbishments
- a spreadsheet for modelling short term / holiday lets

The spreadsheets are the ones I use personally in my own property investments. It's all completely free with no sell on. Just sign up at my website at:

www.essentialproperty.net/playbook-vol-1

Contents

Introduction

There's more to property than buy-to-let and refurbishments. In fact, there are so many different ways to make a profit in property, it's impossible to keep track of them all. It can take years to really get to grips with all the different strategies out there and longer still to master them, to decode the tactics and steps behind other property investors' success. This book is designed to help you shortcut that journey. It's not a blueprint for how to be successful in property – there is no such thing. Instead, it's been written to give an overview of the common factors and typical "plays" behind most property success stories and the techniques these investors are using to make money and build their portfolios. It's designed to broaden your horizons before you get too deep into a particular mode of thinking or go too far down one particular route. It's designed to teach you how to think like a successful property investor.

This book started out life several years ago as my own property journal, a scrapbook of ideas, approaches and unrelated factoids I collected in the course of my own research. As a new investor starting out in property, I was stunned by the variety of ways people were making money and growing their wealth through property. Every investor I met seemed to have their own ways of doing things and their own plan for reaching their goals. Of course, their strategies included all the basic approaches like buy-to-let, flips and refinancing. But there were all kinds of other ways people were growing their wealth too – from creative ways to use their own homes, via multiple flips and taking in lodgers, to niche financing strategies like second mortgage charges and seller financing. I started to keep a log of all these different ideas in my journal. Every book I read, podcast I listened to, or investor I spoke to, if there was a new idea or approach I'd never heard of, it went in the book. That book eventually took on a life of its own and turned into the piece of writing you have before you today.

The Property Investment Playbook is a course designed to give an overview of all the various strategies or plays that UK property investors are using to grow their property portfolios. It's a compilation of the best and smartest techniques out there, covering everything from how to get started to more sophisticated and advanced techniques used by investors with years of experience under their belt. If you're new to property investment, the book will teach you how to get started and all of the basic strategies you'll need to succeed, including the oldies and the goodies like basic buy-to-let and light refurbishments. For experienced investors, I hope the book will challenge you to add a few new plays to your own playbook and expand your repertoire. I hope it also helps you to develop a more creative mindset and to come up with better and more innovative ways to do deals.

The course is split into two parts. Volume 1 is aimed at new property investors and those who've been investing for a few years but still feel they could improve at the basics. Volume 2 is aimed at more experienced property investors, but it's also suitable for anyone looking to learn one or more of the advanced investment techniques typically reserved for experienced investors. Here's a quick overview of what's covered in Volume 1 of the playbook.

In Part One, we'll run through everything you need to know and everything you need to do while you're getting yourself ready to invest. We'll run through how to set your property goals and develop a strategy that works for you, how to get your personal finances in order, and how to put the right team and structures in place around you to maximise your chances of success. In Part Two, we'll cover all the things you can do to build your capital base and the resources you have at your disposal. We'll run through all the things you can do to help you save harder and build deposits quicker and look at some creative ways to use your own home to build equity and generate additional income. We'll also look at how you can use alternative sources of finance to speed up your progress. In Part Three, we'll cover all the core strategies you need to know when you're making your first investments. We'll look at basic buy-to-lets, light refurbishments, and how to flip properties for a profit. These plays are at the heart of most property investors' strategies. We'll also look at some advanced financing techniques and how you can take advantage of joint ventures to speed up your progress. Finally, we'll take a look at some alternative property business models, like short term holiday lets and serviced accommodation.

Everything in this book is geared towards making you a better investor by giving you an overview of the strategies and techniques you can use to build a property business that works for you. In each play, we'll run through things like the keys to success and common pitfalls and mistakes, to increase your chances of success if you put that strategy to work for yourself. We'll also look at when these strategies work best and when they might not work so well. If you're looking to take your strategic thinking to the next level, my hope is that this book will help you do just that. Most of all, I hope that you have fun reading this book and that it opens up your eyes to a vast world of possibilities and encourages you to think just a little bit bigger about what you might achieve with property and how you might go about it.

Robert Heaton
October 2020

How to use this book

A personal note

I wrote this book with my partner Ye for pleasure. We invest in property together, and we both enjoy analysing and understanding the different property strategies and what makes them work – that is, the broader investment principles at play. Before I started writing, I thought the book was going to be all about the different strategies and tactics investors use in pursuit of their goals, which it is. However, it's also about something deeper too. Throughout the book, running through each and every play, is a subtext that calls for creativity. Property isn't usually thought of as a creative endeavour, but I think there's an argument that to really succeed in any field, property included, you have to engage the creative spirit – to use your imagination to help you build something that didn't previously exist. In this sense, I think property can be just as creative as any other field, and I hope this book helps you to unlock some of the joy that springs from the knowledge you've made something of yourself and expressed yourself in an artistic sense too. Writing this book was great fun, and I hope some of the fun rubs off. Mostly, I hope this book helps you to grow as an investor and mature as an individual, and that you're able to share the knowledge you gain and the ideas presented with other investors.

How to read the content

There are no hard and fast rules on how you should read this book. Your level of expertise and your motivation for reading the book will help you determine that. However, if you permit me, I would like to proffer a suggestion. If you're a novice and have little knowledge of property investment and property strategies, or if you've been in property for years but feel there might be gaps in your knowledge, I recommend you study the course from the start, taking each of the plays in order. This book was written with exactly that kind of reader in mind. On the other hand, you can simply use this book as a reference manual, reading only the parts you feel might be relevant to you. The plays are basically self-contained and can be read in isolation, though they will occasionally refer back or forward to other sections of the book. Alternatively, you could simply keep this book as your "coffee table book", dipping into it when you have a spare five minutes with a cup of tea or coffee in hand. It's really up to you.

A window on the world

Each play in the book offers a window on the world, a vignette about some aspect of what it takes to succeed as a property investor. Each one offers either a short summary of a particular tactic or strategy or discusses some kind of fundamental principle that successful investors utilise. When you read each of the plays, I encourage you to think about how you might use that principle or strategy in pursuit of your own goals. Think about the pros and the cons of the play, whether that strategy is suited to your skillset and your experience, and what you would have to do or give up in order to use it in practice.

It's also worth discussing what this book is not, and that's a comprehensive and detailed account of each of the tactics and strategies presented. Each play is simply an outline, and you'll need more details than are presented, if you want to use that play for yourself. There are plenty of other books, blogs, podcasts and courses out there that you can use to fill in the gaps I've left here. This course is designed for breadth, not depth, and you should see it as a jumping-off point into the big, wide world of property and the other resources out there.

I also want to add some guidance for our international readers. Ye and I are both UK property investors, and the plays described in this book were built using our knowledge and experience of investing in the UK. As such, some of the detail included will only be relevant to UK investors. However, I'm confident that the ideas presented are general enough that they could be applied in other property markets around the world too. A good example would be letting out a spare room. The specifics of the Rent a Room Scheme here in the UK will not be relevant to international readers, but the broader idea will be, and with a bit of creative thinking this play could be adapted and applied in other markets. I'd encourage all readers, not just international ones, to think about how they can put their own signature on each idea presented to get the most out of it.

A source of inspiration

My final hope for this book is that it acts as a source of inspiration for everyone who reads it. The day-to-day aspects of property investment and running a rental portfolio can be hard, and the wins are few and far between. I hope that this book can, in its own small way, help make that journey a little bit more fun and keep you motivated to succeed. Anytime you're struggling with the why, anytime you get slapped with an unexpected service charge, anytime you're looking for a new property challenge – I hope this book is one you'll pick off your bookshelf and have a leaf through in search of motivation and encouragement. Above all, I hope this book is a counterpoint to the naysayers and critics who doubt what you're trying to achieve. Remember, in the immortal words of Teddy Roosevelt, nothing worth having was ever achieved without effort.

Basic investment terminology

In other books, you'll find all kinds of background on the different terminology and numerical underpinnings behind property investment. All of this is essential knowledge, but I'm not going to cover it again here, as there simply wouldn't be enough space. If you're looking for further background on the numbers side of property, I've written a whole book on this very topic, called *Essential Property Investment Calculations*, covering all of the calculations, numerical techniques and metrics most property investors use to assess property deals and manage their portfolios. In this book, I've tried to bring in only those details needed to understand the strategies and plays presented and how they work. That being said, there are a few key terms and fundamental metrics you need to know to read this book. Let's recap on some of these now.

Rental yield calculations

Capitalisation rate

Capitalisation rate ("cap rate" for short) is calculated as the annual net operating profit from the rental property divided by the purchase price of the property, assuming the investor buys the property without using a mortgage. Because of this, the profit calculation excludes mortgage costs:

$$Cap\ rate = \frac{Annual\ net\ operating\ profit}{Purchase\ price}$$

$$or$$

$$Cap\ rate = \frac{(Annual\ rental\ income - Annual\ rental\ costs)}{Purchase\ price}$$

We need to include all the other costs associated with running the property, i.e. marketing costs, letting agent fees, repair and maintenance costs, service charges and ground rents, etc. Capitalisation rate gives investors a measure of how good the returns are for the rental property itself, ignoring mortgage financing costs. It allows investors to compare properties on a consistent basis.

Return on investment

Return on investment ("ROI") shows us how our rental profits compare with the actual cash we have invested in the deal. ROI is the annual rental profit from the property divided by the cash you've invested in the deal. If you've bought the property in cash without a mortgage, this is the same as the cap rate, but if you've used a mortgage you'll have put in less of your own cash:

$$ROI = \frac{Annual\ rental\ profit}{Cash\ invested}$$

$$or$$

$$ROI = \frac{(Annual\ rental\ income - Annual\ rental\ costs)}{Cash\ invested}$$

When we carry out the calculation, we need to include all rental costs this time, including any mortgage costs. Equally, when we calculate the cash invested, we need to include all the cash costs of purchasing the property, like our deposit, stamp duty, valuation fees, broker costs, etc. These are all real cash costs that need to be paid upfront, so they should be included in our calculation.

ROI is our best guess at the return we're actually going to achieve on our cash. Because of this, you can even compare it with the potential returns you'd get on non-property investments, e.g. the interest we'd received on a bank account or the dividend yield on a share. It shows you how hard your money is working for you and how this compares with other available investments. For most of the plays in this book, the key number I focus on when analysing returns is the ROI. So, if you only remember one formula, this is the one to choose.

Capital growth

The calculations we've looked at above only consider the rental returns from a property. However, many property investors are also looking for capital growth. Capital growth is the uplift in the value of a property over time. It's an extra source of return for property investors, if they experience some. However, there are no guarantees you'll experience any, and the level of capital growth you can expect is inherently uncertain, as is the timeframe over which it will play out. As such, it's usually best to base your investment decisions on the two metrics we've covered above and see capital growth as more of a nice-to-have. That being said, there are plenty of investors out there who invest mainly with capital growth in mind and who try to pick an area or location where they think the prospects for future growth are strongest. The important thing to remember is that it's the market, not the investor, that controls the general level of capital growth.

Financing and leverage

Leverage is one of those words that property investors throw around all the time. Here they're talking about financial leverage, and by that we simply mean using borrowed money to invest in assets. That is, when we buy a property, we put in some of the money ourselves, and we use borrowed money from a lender or bank to purchase the rest. In short, most properties are bought using mortgages.

The two main types of mortgage you can use to invest in buy-to-let properties are repayment and interest only mortgages. With a repayment mortgage, you pay off a small amount of the loan each month plus some interest. By the end of the loan term, you'll have paid off the loan in full. With an interest only mortgage, you pay just the interest on the borrowed money each month. At the end of the loan term, you still need to pay back the original amount borrowed, so you'll need a plan for how to pay this back. With a repayment mortgage, because you pay off the loan gradually over time, your monthly repayments will be higher than with an interest only mortgage.

Payments on an interest only mortgage

It's simple to calculate the monthly repayments on an interest only mortgage. If the loan amount is A and our interest rate is i, we calculate this as follows:

$$Monthly\ payment = (A \times i)/12$$

For example, if you borrow £100,000 at a 3% p.a. interest rate, the payments will be £100,000 × 3% ÷ 12 which equals £250 per month.

Payments on a repayment mortgage

To estimate the payments on a repayment mortgage, we need a more involved formula. Here we have A as the loan amount, i as the interest rate, and T as the term (length) of the mortgage. We calculate our monthly repayments as follows:

$$Monthly\ payment = \frac{1}{12} \times \left(\frac{A \times i}{(1 - (1+i)^{-T})} \right)$$

For example, if you take out a loan of £100,000 for a term of 25 years at a 3% p.a. interest rate, the monthly payments will be as follows:

$$\frac{1}{12} \times \left(\frac{£100,000 \times 0.03}{(1 - (1.03)^{-25})} \right) = £479$$

For our technical readers, the formula above assumes (for simplicity) that your mortgage payments are paid annually in arrears – that is, all at once at the end of the year. In practice, you'll make payments on a monthly basis throughout the year, and your payments will actually be slightly less that the estimate provided by the formula above.

Interest only versus repayment

Property investors typically opt for interest only mortgages. Their thinking is that it requires lower monthly payments, so it improves their cash flow position. The investor then has a choice of whether to use the extra cash flow to pay down some of the outstanding loan balance, thereby reducing the amount they owe, or put it towards their next property purchase instead. If you're not overly comfortable with the general idea of debt, then a repayment mortgage might appear the safer choice. However, it's really a matter of personal preference and your tolerance for risk. What's more, if your plan is to grow a large portfolio, you'll likely want to opt for interest only and reinvest that extra cash flow. As such, throughout this book, we'll assume you take out interest only mortgages to finance your property investments, unless stated otherwise.

Wrapping it up

That's really all the calculations and basic terminology you need to read this book. If you're new to property investment and the short recap above wasn't enough, you can check out my book, *Essential Property Investment Calculations*, or one of the introductory property books out there for more background on the numbers side of things. With that recap out of the way, hit the lights and cue the music – it's time for the main attraction.

Part One : Getting yourself ready to invest

Play # 1 – Get straight on your property goals

Ever since the buy-to-let boom of the late 1990s, Tom had been involved in property. At the start, he'd followed his nose and had some early success, building a portfolio of five rental properties in just a few years. Since then, he'd changed his approach a number of times, dabbling in everything from HMOs and holiday lets to refurbs and property flips. What he'd ended up with was a mishmash of properties with no clear theme. Now, just ten years from retirement, he was starting to wonder where all this was headed and if he was still on track for that early retirement he'd always dreamed about. What he needed was to get straight on his property goals, and fast.

Finding your North Star

It might seem strange to start a book on property investment with a section on goal setting, but having clear objectives is crucial to success in property (or any other area of life) and it's often overlooked. Every successful investor I know has clear goals – a set of core aims and objectives that define what success looks like to them. These goals act as their North Star, helping to guide them where they want to go and keeping them well-oriented when life knocks them around. In the words of Lewis Carroll, who knows a thing or two about falling down rabbit holes, if you don't know where you're going, any road will get you there.

Before you start investing in property, it's important to get clear on what you want and what you want property to do for you. Not enough people set their goals before they start investing, and they're opening themselves up to disappointment and missing out on an opportunity to unlock the transformational power of goals. A clear set of goals can help keep you motivated when things get tough, prevent you wasting time on the latest craze, and help you to evaluate the opportunities that cross your path, whether that be investing in a particular property or screening out certain investment approaches. Over the longer term, goals allow you to stretch yourself further than you thought possible; they also give you the permission to celebrate your wins and achievements. In this section, we're going to look at what makes a great goal and how to set property goals that tap into a deeper meaning or purpose. We'll also look at a simple process for turning those goals into long term action.

What makes a great goal?

There's lots of literature out there on goal setting and on what makes a great goal. A quick rummage around the internet and you'll find lots of discussion on goals needing to be SMART – that is, specific, measurable, achievable, and so on. And there are plenty of other acronyms out there too. It's all great stuff, of course, but for me, nothing saps my enthusiasm quicker than a clever sounding checklist I'm obliged to work through. As such, I'm going to throw all that out of the window and focus on the two key criteria I think make a great goal. For me, great goals need to be *measurable* and *meaningful*.

Setting measurable goals

The old adage that what gets measured gets managed is as true for property goals as it is in any other walk of life. In order to set a great goal, we need to pick a target that's measurable. Goals like "I want to retire by the time I'm 50" or "I want to achieve financial freedom" are certainly aspirational, but without some kind of yardstick to measure our progress, they're difficult to track and they lack the kind of concreteness that helps motivate daily action. The simple remedy for this is to set your goal around something quantifiable and measurable.

For most property investors, the best metric to use here is monthly cash flow or monthly profit. With enough thought and a bit of careful calculation, a goal to "retire early" or "achieve financial freedom" can be expressed as a measurable goal to "generate £2,000 per month from my property portfolio" in order that you might retire early or have the freedom to quit your job if you wish. It's possible, though I don't see it often in practice, to set measurable goals around the amount of wealth you want to accumulate through property. It's really up to you.

Setting meaningful goals

Now we've got a handle on the measurable part, it's worth thinking about how we can make sure the goals we set ourselves are meaningful too. The answer to that lies in tying our goals and objectives to some wider aspect of our lives. That is, we need to pick an income figure or a wealth target that means something to us. Take a monthly income target, for example – this could represent the amount of income you would need each month in order to survive if both you and your partner lost your jobs. Likewise, a wealth target could represent a particular sum of money you want to leave to your children, perhaps to buy each of them a home. Tying our property goals to our life goals in some way is what matters.

Property dreamlining

A useful tool for defining a meaningful income figure is a property dreamline. The idea of a "dreamline" was popularised by Tim Ferriss in his book *The 4-hour Work Week*. It's one that works well for property investors looking to gauge the level of income they'll need to buy their dream lifestyle. The exercise starts out with a simple budgeting exercise to build an estimate of the monthly income you'd need to cover your everyday living expenses. For many investors, this is a figure in the range £1,500 to £2,500 per month, depending on where you live, the size of your family, and your other life commitments. On top of this, you then add elements of your dream lifestyle and convert each of these into a monthly cost. For example, say you wanted to spend three months of each year travelling at a cost of £4,000 per month. This is a total cost of £12,000, or £1,000 per month, that you can add to your living expenses. You should add in two or three key items here.

Finally, you can subtract off any income you still expect to be generating as part of your dream lifestyle – yes, believe it or not, many people are still happy to do some work as part of their dream lifestyle, albeit they often hope to be doing this more on their own terms. The end result of this exercise is a monthly income figure you want to generate from property, the price tag on your dream lifestyle. It should be meaningful for you, and it should be aspirational. If you're interested in doing an exercise like this, make sure you check out the free resources section at the back of this book for details of how to get hold of a copy of my dreamlining spreadsheet and give it a go.

Turning big goals into long term action

Okay, so we've picked a lofty goal like being financial free, and we've developed a monthly income target to go with it, but we're not quite done yet. The next and arguably the most important step in the process is to break that big goal into bite-sized chunks. In their excellent book, *Switch*, authors Chip Heath and Dan Heath talk about "shrinking the change". The idea is that the only way to get to your big goals is to accomplish smaller goals first and to build up momentum. But what does this mean for your property goals?

Well, say your big, lofty goal was to generate £3,000 per month from property to support your dream lifestyle and take care of your family. Also, suppose, based on your current financial resources, your savings rate, and your chosen property strategy, that you think this will take around eight to ten years to achieve. Well, eight to ten years is an awfully long time to stay focussed, and it will be better for your resolve if you focus on what you need to achieve in the first two to three years of that plan, rather than tackling the whole thing in one sitting and getting overwhelmed.

Let's look at how this could work for the example above. Suppose you have some savings built up already that you're willing to deploy immediately. In this case, your one-year goals might become something like the following:

- buy one buy-to-let property giving a cash flow of £250 per month
- save £30,000 to put towards a second buy-to-let property in year two

Then, looking further ahead, you might decide that the following goals will get you to where you need to be by the end of year two:

- buy a second buy-to-let property giving a cash flow of £250 per month
- save £40,000 to put towards a third buy-to-let property in year three
- renovate and sell your own home for a £40,000 profit you can reinvest

Don't worry too much about the specifics of the goals above at this stage, they're for illustration purposes only. The key point here is that you should break down your big goal into manageable sub-goals with a shorter time horizon. In practice, most people find two or three years works well for these shorter-term goals – it's long enough to be meaningful, but short enough to keep you focussed. Likewise, you can break down those annual goals into monthly and even weekly goals to keep you on-track throughout the year.

Common pitfalls and mistakes

The main pitfalls and mistakes that can arise with goal setting are all to do with mindset. Here are a few of the most common ones:

- Not pitching goals at the right level – If you're too ambitious and asking too much of yourself, you'll lose motivation when your goals drift by. Likewise, if your goals aren't stretching enough, you might be inclined to slack off.

- Not thinking long term – People tend to overestimate what can be done in one year and underestimate what can be done in five or ten years. Make sure your big goal is challenging enough.
- Having a get rich quick mindset – If you're getting into property because you think it will make you an overnight millionaire, you might be disappointed. It takes effort and commitment over the long term to make it.
- Changing tack too often – Lots of investors spend time chasing the latest fad, something that's been dubbed "shiny object syndrome". Change direction too often, and it'll be harder to get where you're trying to go.
- Not tracking goals over time – If you have no way of tracking your goals and holding yourself to account, your goals will likely go unmet. Make sure you have a system in place for checking in on these from time to time.

Finally, it's worth saying that by far the biggest mistake most investors make around goal setting is not setting any goals in the first place. At the start of your property journey, when you're getting ready to invest, you'll have plenty of time to get straight on your goals and get clear on what you want. Make sure you know what you want from property and what you want property to do for you.

Play # 2 – Get yourself out of debt (personal finance tip # 1)

Helen had long aspired to become a property investor. She loved anything DIY-related, and she saw the benefits of building up a second income outside of her corporate day job, but her personal finances were all over the place. She'd become better at saving as she'd gotten older, but her lack of financial discipline in the past meant she still had some debt – a little on credit cards, a personal loan she hadn't yet paid off, and student debt from her university days. Before she even thought about property investment, she needed to get her personal finances in order and clear away her debts.

Taking a step back

To state the obvious, property investment is a form of investment. In order to succeed, you'll need capital to invest – lots of it in fact. So, you'll want to make sure you direct all the money you can spare towards your investments and avoid unnecessary payouts to anyone else. For many people, that means the first step in their property journey might actually be a step backwards – getting themselves out of debt and back in the black. As in all walks of life, sometimes it's necessary to take a step back in order to move forward.

Let's face it, debt has become part of our culture. In our modern, connected world, you can take out a credit card or extend your overdraft at the click of a button, without ever leaving the house. This easy access to credit has made it all too easy to get into debt. In fact, it's expected that most of us will carry some level of debt in our everyday lives, whether that be in the form of student loans, car leasing schemes, bank overdrafts or credit cards. But it doesn't have to be that way. It is possible to go through life without taking on debt, and that should be your aim, as every pound you save in interest payments paying off your debt can be put towards your property investments. In this section, we're going to look at what you need to know about debt, and we'll walk through a simple five-step process you can use to pay off your existing debts.

What you need to know about debt

At the heart of our debt problem lies our need for instant gratification. Borrowing in all its forms allows us to buy something earlier than we might have otherwise, something we haven't got the money for right now. But that doesn't come for free. We also end up paying the lender for the privilege of this early access. With that in mind, let's take a look at some key things you need to know about debt.

Most debt is bad debt

There's lots of literature out there about the difference between good debt and bad debt. The general idea is that if the debt you take on helps you generate extra income and increase your net worth, it can be considered positive, and it's seen as *good debt*. Examples might include a student loan, if the course you're studying increases your earnings potential, a loan to buy equipment to start a business, or borrowing to buy an appreciating asset like a property. Likewise, it's generally seen as *bad debt* if that debt doesn't help you generate extra income in some way. So, bad debt includes any borrowing to buy consumable goods and services like clothes and holidays and depreciating assets like cars. Not all debt is that easy to classify – so if you're in doubt, simply remember that most debt is bad debt.

All debt brings risk

Whether a particular debt is good debt or bad debt can sometimes be a matter of opinion. One thing is always true, however – all debt brings risk. Every form of borrowing, whether that be a mortgage, a car loan, or a credit card, creates an obligation to make loan repayments and makes your position more fragile. If you suddenly find yourself with a loss in income, those repayment obligations will still be there. That's why debt, even good debt, needs to be handled with care, and it's why you should think long and hard about every borrowing decision, even in the context of property investment where leverage is commonplace.

Debt makes other people rich

When a lender lends you money, they do it because it makes them money – via interest payments on loans and mortgages and through fees and late payment charges with overdrafts and credit cards. In this way, debt makes other people rich and it keeps you poor. The defence against this is to stay out of debt wherever possible, and that means paying in cash or on debit card for most things in your life. The one exception to this is perhaps a mortgage on your own home, as most people will struggle to save enough upfront to purchase their home outright. The key thing here is not to buy a home that's too big for you – the larger the home, the larger the mortgage, and the money you spend meeting interest payments is money you could have put towards investment instead.

A five-step process for paying off your debts

What if you're already carrying some existing debt that you want to get rid of? Let's look at a simple five-step process you can use to secure a debt-free lifestyle. I've borrowed this process from a number of personal finance experts. If you're in debt at the moment and you're keen to get debt-free, make sure you check out some of the excellent podcasts and blog articles out there as a follow up to this.

1. Budget for debt repayment

The first step is a simple budgeting exercise to work out how much you can put towards paying down your debts each month. This should be as much as humanly possible. You should be aiming to find every pound you can, and that might mean not eating out this month or getting a second job to earn extra income. You should also think about whether there are things you own that you could sell. We're not messing around here, we're serious about paying down that debt quickly.

2. Build an emergency buffer

Before you actually start paying down any of your debts, you should use that first slug of cash to build an emergency buffer fund of between £500 to £1,000 which you'll hold in a separate account. This fund is only to be used in a real emergency, and it's there to stop you taking out any new forms of debt, like new credit cards. The rules of the emergency fund are simple: (1) if you have to use it, you'll top it up again first before paying down any further debts; (2) if you're doing this as a couple, you can't touch it unless you both agree; (3) you have to sleep on it before you make a decision to use it. The psychology behind the emergency buffer fund is actually quite simple – you need to get used to living within your means, and you need to break the habit of turning to new debt in times of crisis.

3. List out all of your debts

The next step in the process is to list out all your debts in order of size, with the smallest at the top and largest at the bottom. The only exception to this is payday loans, which are expensive and which you should put at the top of your list.

4. Pay off the smallest debt first

So, we've built an emergency buffer and listed our debts from smallest to largest. The next step in the process is to make the minimum payments on all but the smallest of our debts, and to blast the smallest debt with whatever is left in our debt repayment budget. You're going to carry on doing this month after month until the smallest debt is paid off. Then you're going to close down that account and make sure you never use it again. This last step is critical to your success, as it creates a feeling of progress and acts as an important psychological barrier to taking on more debt again in the future.

5. Build momentum as you go

Finally, you're going to repeat this process for each of your debts, working from smallest to largest. With every debt you clear, you'll build momentum. Each debt you clear creates extra budget (the minimum payment on the next debt up) that you can put towards debt repayment, meaning your process will get quicker and quicker over time until you're debt-free and in the clear.

Some final thoughts

In many ways, the process I've described above doesn't make logical sense. You might be wondering, for example, why you wouldn't pay down the debt with the highest interest rate first. And that's because this process is designed to work from a human perspective, not to give the best financial outcome. By working from the smallest debt to the largest, you're giving yourself some quick wins early on in the fight, and this will help keep you focussed and motivated for longer. The other side effect is that by the end of this process, you'll be used to paying yourself first, and all the money you were using to repay debts can instead be put towards your investment goals. The process will teach you financial discipline, and it will give you the resolve and determination to follow through over the long term.

Reversal

Having said all of that, are there are times when it makes more sense to invest rather than pay down debt? There are a couple of different angles to this. From a financial perspective, if you can get a higher return on investment by investing your money than the interest cost on your debt, then you'll increase your wealth faster by investing first, then paying down debt later. Let's take a simple example.

Say you have £30,000 in savings and your two choices are as follows: (a) invest in a buy-to-let property that will generate an ROI of 6% or £1,800 per year; (b) pay down £30,000 of debt with an annual interest cost of 3% or £900. In this case, you'll be better off financially if you choose to invest – the money you earn from the investment under option (a) can be used to pay the interest on the loan and leave you with £900 in cash to spare at the end of the year. In many cases, you'd be right to go down this route.

My main caveat to this would be if keeping the debt in place will affect your credit rating and prevent you from borrowing in the first place, in which case you may have no choice but to pay off the debt first. It's also worth pointing out that certain forms of borrowing, in particular student loans, are conditional – that is, they don't need to be repaid until your earnings rise above a certain level. In this case, provided the ROI on the investment is higher than the interest on the loan, i.e. that it makes sound financial sense, there's a strong financial argument for using your savings to invest, rather than pay off the loan. Ultimately, it's up to you to decide what makes sense for you.

Play # 3 – Work to a budget (personal finance tip # 2)

At the end of each month, Penny would check her online banking and see how much she could transfer to her savings account. Usually, it wasn't much. She was frustrated with herself and her progress. When she discussed this with colleagues, they mentioned ideas like setting herself a monthly budget and paying herself first. Budgeting she'd heard about, but didn't know how to do it; paying herself first was not something she'd come across before, but it sounded like a good idea. Over the next few months, she educated herself on these ideas and managed to implement a savings regime that turned out to be the start of her property journey.

Spending less than you earn

To be successful in property you need capital to invest, and you won't get far without a strong savings mentality. The core principle at work here is spending less than you earn. This is not an easy thing to do, but without it nothing else is possible. In my experience, the only way to spend less than you earn is to set up and stick to a monthly budget. So, although nobody gets excited about it, setting and working to a budget is essential for good money management, and it's the only practical way to hit your savings and investment goals.

There are lots of things that prevent people doing this kind of budgeting. The biggest barrier is often a lack of knowledge – that is, people don't actually know how to go about it. Another common hurdle is the emotional barrier that comes with worrying about what you might find when you dig into your finances. I call this the "head-in-the-sand" approach. Neither of these are good reasons for not budgeting, so don't let them hold you back. In this section, we're going to look at what makes a good budget and at a three-step budgeting process you can use. If you weren't excited about budgeting before, I hope you soon will be.

What makes a good budget?

The budget you set yourself is there to help you take control of your finances and meet your savings target. In order for a budget to be useful, it needs to meet three basic criteria.

It needs to be proactive

A good budget needs to be forward-looking, not backward-looking. Your budget is a plan for how and where you will spend your money in the month to come, and it's there to actively help you decide where your money will go. If all you're doing is working out where you already spent your cash, that's not budgeting.

It must be written down

If your budget is not written down in some way, then it's just not going to happen. It doesn't matter whether your budget is written on a piece of paper and kept in a filing cabinet or set out in an Excel spreadsheet. You can use whatever format works for you, just make sure it's more than a vague idea in your mind.

It should be easy to work with

Your budget is your financial plan, and every plan needs to be adjusted. Whatever format you use to track your finances, it should be easy to work with and it should be a tool you enjoy using. That is, it needs to have a low barrier to entry, as you'll be busting it out a couple of times each month to track your progress.

A three-step budgeting process

Now that we understand the basics, we're going to look at a simple budgeting process you can use to track your monthly finances. There's no secret sauce or magic ingredient here, just some simple maths and plain old common sense.

Getting set up correctly

Before we get into the process, it's important to set your bank accounts up in the right way. You'll need three accounts for this particular system.

1. Bills account – Set it up so that all your bills, including your rent or mortgage, council tax, and all your utility bills, are paid out of this one account.
2. Spending account – Use a separate account for all your day-to-day spending, including spending on groceries, nights outs, and any entertainment.
3. Savings account – This last account could be any kind of savings account, whether that be an ISA or a Premium Bonds account with NS&I.

These three accounts will be the bedrock of our budgeting system, and we'll use them to keep our system in check and instil some financial discipline.

Step 1 – Setting your monthly budget

Ahead of each payday, or at the month end if you're paid weekly, you're going to sit down for an hour and actively set your budget for the following month. You need to decide how much money you're going to allocate to each of your three accounts. For the bills account, this should be enough money to cover your rent or mortgage, your council tax, and all your bills, and it should stay fairly stable from one month to the next. For the spending account, we then decide how much we're going to need to cover living expenses like groceries, travel, eating out, and entertainment. Make sure you allow for any known one-off expenses that month, e.g. school trips or new clothing. What's left goes into your savings account – if there's not enough to hit your target, then see what spending you can cut.

Let's take a walk through a simple example. Suppose you and your partner bring home a combined £4,250 each month after tax. Your rent and your utilities come to around £1,250 each month, so we're going to set that aside in our bills account. Next, we come to our spending budget. You normally spend around £800 per month (£200 per week) on groceries and eating out and £100 on travel. In addition, next month you need to attend your brother's wedding, so you'll need an extra £100 to cover the cost of petrol and a wedding gift. In total, you have a budget of £1,000 for the spending account, leaving you £2,000 for your savings account. If you'd hoped to save more than £2,000 this month, then you'll have to scale back your spending in some way in order to achieve this.

Step 2 – What to do on payday

The process you need to follow on payday should be pretty straightforward and mechanical. When the money hits your account, you need to allocate it as per your budget. That is, you should keep enough money in your bills account to cover the monthly bills, and you should transfer the monthly spending budget to your spending account. The rest of the money gets transferred to your savings account. This last step is an important one. Don't be tempted to leave that savings money hanging around in one of the other accounts, make sure it's tucked away somewhere that's harder to access and where you won't be tempted to dip into it if something goes wrong over the course of the month.

Step 3 – Use micro-adjustments to stay on track

The last step in our process is a weekly check-in on our spending account to see whether we're still on track. This should be quick and easy, and it should take no more than ten minutes. The simple question you want to ask yourself each week is whether there's enough money left in the spending account to get you through to the end of the month, or whether you need to make some adjustments to your planned spending in some way. This is where your budgeting comes into its own, and it's also where the hard choices get made.

Let's take a closer look at this using the example we developed above. Suppose you check in on your spending account two weeks into the month, and you find there's only £350 of the £1,000 left. That feels a bit on the low side, but let's work through the numbers. Your partner bought her monthly train pass, so that's the £100 on travel gone. You've also spent £400 on groceries and eating out (half of the £800 budgeted), £100 to attend the wedding, and £50 on a new pair of shoes when yours started leaking. At this point, everything but the £50 on shoes was budgeted. So, you know that to stay on-track, you need to cut your budget for groceries and eating out in the final two weeks by £50 from £400 to £350. Here's the micro-adjustment. To do this, you decide to get an M&S gastro pub ready meal for the next two Fridays, rather than spending £35 each Friday eating out.

Common pitfalls and mistakes

The main pitfalls and mistakes that can arise with this kind of budgeting are when you're not honest with yourself. Here are a few common ones:

- Not being open with your partner – Your partner will have different visibility on what's coming up and on any one-off expenses that might be needed. Make sure all of these are included in your monthly spending budget. Both you and your partner need to be fully committed to the budget.
- Playing mental accounting games – It's the last Friday of the month and you get paid next Tuesday, but there's not enough in the spending account for a night out. That's okay, you'll stick it on your credit card, right? Wrong. These kind of mental accounting games will get you into all kinds of hot water.
- Not knowing why you're doing it – There will always be unexpected costs, and family, friends and work colleagues have a way of adding to these. If you don't know why you're doing it, it will be harder to make the difficult choices you'll need to make to stay on track.

This final point is the key to keeping yourself on track over the long term. You need a strong reason and a clear goal to stick with this kind of financial discipline over a period of months and years. If you're not clear on your goals yet, make sure you read through play # 1 which is all about goal setting.

Redux

The final thing to say on budgeting is that you can and you should get ruthless with every last line item of spending. If you've never done this kind of exercise before, then print out your bank and credit card statements for the last six to twelve months and go through them line by line to work out what discretionary spending you can cut out. Do you really need Netflix and Amazon Prime? Pick one. Could you change your mobile contract to a SIM-only deal that costs less than £10 per month? Could you buy yourself a second-hand car in cash for £3,000, rather than signing up for that expensive car leasing scheme. Be hard on yourself. Every last pound you cut is another pound you can put towards saving and building that portfolio of investment properties. As my pop used to say, look after the pennies, and the pounds will look after themselves.

Play # 4 – Clean up your credit score (personal finance tip # 3)

Lorenzo had saved hard for his first deposit, sourced and negotiated a great buy-to-let deal, and he was about to pull the trigger, but things started to go wrong when he couldn't secure a mortgage. In the past, Lorenzo's personal finances had been less than good; he'd been in and out of debt several times before he'd got his finances in order, and his credit report was testament to that. With the help of a broker, he managed to get the deal back on track, but not without a lot of stress and some sleepless nights. There were a limited number of lenders willing to finance the deal, so he ended up paying a higher interest rate, but at least he got the deal over the line.

Why credit scores matter

Credit scores are a decision-making tools lenders use to help them anticipate how likely you are to repay a loan. Lenders use credit scores to assess the risk that you won't be able to repay a loan on the terms agreed, and so they can be an important factor in whether you're able to raise finance for investment.

It's certainly true that later on in your property investment journey, your ability to borrow will likely be dictated more by the health and profitability of your existing portfolio, but early on, when lenders don't have a lot to go on, your credit score can be important. Having a good credit score can make the difference between qualifying for a loan or not, and, depending on the interest rate attached to that loan, it could save you hundreds of pounds each month. As such, early on in your property journey, it makes sense to do everything you can to keep your credit score and your ability to borrow in good shape.

Six ways to improve your credit score

In this section, we're going to take a quick canter through some of the things you can do to improve your credit score and put yourself in the best position before you start looking for finance. It's worth saying that if your credit score is in really bad shape, you might want to speak to an expert on this rather than going it alone. There are plenty of advisory services that can support you with this.

1. Get hold of your credit reports

The first step to improving your credit score is to find out what your credit report actually says. You can get hold a copy of your credit report free of charge from an online service like Credit Karma or Experian. Once you've got hold of a copy, you should go through it line by line and check it for accuracy. Check the status of any loans, your account balances, and your payment history. Make sure that all your personal details are correct and up to date with no errors.

2. Dispute any errors

If you do find any errors or mistakes on your credit report, you should try to get them removed. In order to do this, you'll need to raise a dispute with the provider. The process for raising a dispute is normally straightforward and can be done via your online account. You'll need to file a separate dispute for each error and with each provider, providing some supporting documentation as evidence.

3. Automate your payments

The single biggest factor affecting your credit score is your payment history, in particular that for bank loans and credit cards. Your score will take into account both the number and severity of any missed or late payments, so you should do everything you can to ensure you make all payments on time. Where possible, you could consider automating these payments through direct debits, if you're comfortable with these. You might even get a discount for paying this way.

4. Lower your credit utilisation

Your *credit utilisation* is the ratio of how much credit you're using versus how much you have available. The lower this ratio the better. Lenders prefer to see that you're not using too much of your credit limit, as that suggests you're relying on credit for your everyday living expenses, which makes you a higher risk. Make sure you keep this ratio below 25% and below 5% for the best credit scores. You can lower this figure by paying off any big balances.

5. Don't open any new accounts

In general, lenders prefer to see that you haven't opened any new accounts in the last six months. Too many new accounts increases your obligations, making you potentially less likely to meet further commitments. Opening even a single new account can impact your credit score, so try not to open more than one or two accounts in the space of six months to limit the impact of this factor. You should also be careful about applying for too many financial products at one time, as each one leaves a "hard" credit search on your report that other lenders can see.

6. Make sure you're on the electoral roll

This one might sound a little odd, but making sure you're on the electoral roll can improve your credit score. To lenders, that time on the electoral roll helps prove your presence at your current home address and is suggestive of a stable lifestyle and responsible behaviour that is less likely to result in non-payment. The longer you're registered to vote at an address, the more this factor will improve, but you should start to see an improvement in your credit score after a year and a half of being on the electoral roll. By the time you've reached six years or so, you'll have maxed out the benefit of this particular factor.

Further reading and useful resources

There are plenty of good articles and blog posts out there on how to improve your credit score. In addition, Credit Karma and Experian both offer free credit reports if you sign up to their online service. These free reports give you tips on the kinds of things you can do to improve your credit score. Often this is as much a matter of good financial hygiene as it is a serious exercise in paying down your debts, so get organised and see what actions you can take to improve your score. What else have you got to do while you're saving for that next deposit?

Play # 5 – Invest in your personal development

Like many other property investors, Emma wished she'd got started sooner. She'd first looked into buy-to-let back in 2016, as a way of generating extra income for her family and reducing their reliance on her job. But as a higher rate taxpayer, she'd been put off by the changes to mortgage interest relief, and her research stopped there. It wasn't until a couple of years later, when she came across an article about using a limited company to invest, that her interest was reignited. Over the next six months, she read all the materials she could get her hands on and listened to hours of podcasts on her 45 minute daily commutes. Late in 2018, she made her first investment, followed by one more in 2019 and another in 2020. She still wished she'd started sooner.

The importance of education

Whether you're just starting out in property or a seasoned professional, there's always more to learn. The property landscape is constantly evolving, and just because your knowledge was up to date yesterday, doesn't mean it will be tomorrow. And one of the most important things you can build is a personal development mindset – that is, a constant desire to get better at what you do and improve your ways of working. In this section, we're going to look at the four pillars of property knowledge that will support your investment journey and at some of the ways you might go about improving your knowledge.

The four pillars of property knowledge

It's useful to think about your strengths and weaknesses across different areas of property. This can help you put together a personal training plan to improve your knowledge or decide where you might need to partner with someone else due to a lack of experience. Here are my four pillars of property knowledge.

1. Strategy – There are lots of different strategies out there and you should aim to develop a working knowledge of them all. That way, when an opportunity presents itself, you'll know whether it's right for you and how to take advantage of it. That's what this book is all about.

2. Financial – Investing in your financial education is key to your success as an investor, whether that be reviewing deals, developing an investment case, how to raise capital, financial and management accounting, or the intricacies of property tax law. There's enough leaning in here for a lifetime.

3. Legal and compliance – Even if you're going to partner with a letting agent, you still need a good enough working knowledge of tenant law and the legal aspects of property to ask the right questions. This is an area that's constantly changing, so you need to keep up to date and stay compliant.

4. Systems and processes – Property is relatively old-fashioned in many ways, with seemingly no end to the bits of paper that need signing and posting back. You should be constantly challenging yourself on how you can improve your systems and processes to make your operation more efficient.

Yes, there are other ways you can think about your development needs, but the framework above has served me well in the past. Once a year, usually in the twilight zone between Christmas and the New Year, my partner and I set aside some time to draw up a personal training plan for the year ahead. We think about where our knowledge might be a little rusty and what we can do to address it. We also think about any completely new areas we want to develop in the coming year that would support our property goals. Then we put it all down in writing so that we have something to check back to during the year to see what progress we've made and what we still need to do to stay on-track.

How to educate yourself

There are lots of different ways to get educated about property investment. Here are just a few of my favourites.

Books and audiobooks

If you're an avid reader like me, then books are a great way to learn. There are some truly excellent books out there covering all the different aspects of property investment, be that learning about a particular strategy or educating yourself about the latest tax rules. Books are also a really economical way of learning. For less than the price of a night out, you have all the author's knowledge set out in an easily digestible form that you can come back to time and again.

Courses

In general, I'm not a big fan of property courses, at least not the expensive type. My advice would be to make the most of any free or inexpensive resources first and then to see if you still feel the need to attend a course after all that. If you're hoping to self-manage and looking for courses on the legal and procedural side of letting out properties, organisations like the National Residential Landlords Association offer some great courses, online and in-person, that are not too costly and will teach you all of this.

Podcasts and videos

This has to be one of my favourite ways to learn. There are hundreds of hours of free podcasts and online videos out there that cover every aspect of property investment, including some of the niche strategies you'll be promised on those expensive courses. Podcasts are often put out there every week, so they're a great way to stay up to date on the latest changes, and they're great for motivation and feeling like you're part of a community. If you have a long commute and time to kill, why not use that time productively.

Networking

If you like to learn from others, then networking is a great way to learn. You can do this in-person at some of the excellent property networking events out there, and you can also network online via one of the property forums. It's a little harder to learn in a structured way using networking, but it's hard to find a substitute for hearing what other investors are up to first-hand. The forums in particular can be a great way to get answers to any really niche property questions you have that you just can't find answers to elsewhere.

Masterminds

A mastermind is a peer-to-peer mentoring group that's used to help people solve their problems through input and advice from the other members of the group. Masterminds are a great way to keep you motivated, to get feedback from other investors on the biggest challenges you face, and to hold yourself accountable for meeting your goals. They tend to work best with more experienced property investors with a few years under their belt.

Shadowing

It's not talked about very often in a property context, but shadowing is ubiquitous in the business world. Shadowing a more experienced property investor can be a great way to learn. If you've never done a flip before, why not ask an experienced flipper if you can shadow them on their next project, all the way from finding the opportunity to fixing up the property ready for a sale. It's the next best thing to actually doing the project yourself, and you'll learn so much from watching all the action live and in technicolour. There really is no substitute.

Self-reflection

Finally, we come to the most underestimated form of learning – self-reflection. That's right, setting aside some time periodically, perhaps once a month or once a quarter, to think about what's gone right for you in property and what's gone wrong is extremely valuable. You should be looking to unpick the reasons why things that went wrong happened and what you can do to prevent them from happening again. Likewise, if something's worked out well, think about how you can reproduce that in the future.

Reversal

There's a certain type of investor (you know who you are) that always feels they need just a little bit more knowledge and education before they can get started. If you suffer from "analysis paralysis" and are struggling to take your first steps in property, then more education might not be the remedy. Yes, it's good to be cautious, and education is certainly a way to reduce your risk and maximise your chances of success, but if you never make any moves at all, then you've already lost. If you've read all the books, listened to all the podcasts, saved up for several deposits, and you still haven't taken action, this might well apply to you. The only cure for this is to take action. Start small and don't put all your eggs in one basket, but do make a move. You owe it to yourself.

Play # 6 – How to decide on your property strategy

Asha's superpower was numbers and coding. He worked in the tech industry and spent his days designing algorithms for all kinds of online businesses, a skill he put to good use in property too. A number of years ago, he designed a web-scraping tool that scanned the internet for investment opportunities and below market value (BMV) properties. The tool had been successful and helped him to spot some great buy-to-let properties in cities he would never have considered. His superpower wasn't a total game-changer – he still had to work hard and save those deposits, but it did help him build his portfolio faster. If he had to put a number on it, probably around 20% faster.

Turning your goals into a strategy

As Michael Porter of Harvard Business School said, "the essence of strategy is choosing what not to do". At the heart of Porter's view of the business world is the concept of trade-offs. In a world of unlimited resources without trade-offs, there would be no need for choice and no need for strategy. But we live in the real world. Our resources are limited, and on a long enough timeline, the survival rate for everyone drops to zero. So, we're going to need a strategy, and quick.

Although it might sound like rather a grand term, a strategy is nothing more than a plan to achieve your long-term goals. We've already looked at how to set your property goals in our first play; we even touched on how to turn those goals into long term action. In this section, we're going to look at how to turn your goals into a strategy that works for you, and we'll do that by looking at some of the key questions you should ask yourself when you're creating that plan.

Pick a strategy that's right for you

Throughout this book, we'll look at lots of property ideas, approaches, and tactics that you can use to reach your property goals. These ideas are neither good nor bad in themselves, but they might be better or worse for you depending or your goals and your specific circumstances. For example, the play that achieves the best ROI may be no good for you, if it requires lots of spare time to achieve it and if you're time poor. We're going to keep things pretty high-level, rather than consider specific investment approaches – that's the job of the rest of this book. Here I'm going to cover the five questions you should ask yourself when you're deciding on your property strategy.

1. What's your timeframe?

If you've followed the advice of play # 1, you'll have set some goals that are both measurable and meaningful. One of the key factors in determining your property strategy is your timeframe for achieving those goals. For example, if your goal is to generate £2,500 per month in rental profits within five years and you expect to have £200,000 to invest over this period, you're unlikely to achieve this with basic buy-to-let investments, and you'll need to look at another approach.

2. How much capital can you invest?

You should think about how much capital you have to invest, both in the near term and over the longer term via additional savings. The amount of capital you have to invest is a key determinant in how quickly you can build your portfolio and whether certain plays are open to you in the first place. For example, it may be possible to secure a discount and buy below market value if you buy in cash, but that's only useful to you if you have that cash available.

3. How much time do you have?

Each investment approach will have its own time requirements. If you're time poor and working 80 hours a week in the city, certain higher yielding strategies like houses in multiple occupation ("HMOs") or self-management of basic buy-to-lets might be off the table. You need to be honest with yourself about the amount of time you have available, and you need to think about what trade-offs you're willing to make.

4. What's your risk tolerance?

Each investor will have their own view of what's risky and each investor will need to get comfortable with the risks inherent in the projects they're taking on. For a conservative investor who's not a big fan of debt, sticking to a moderate amount of leverage and investing in buy-to-lets in areas with high tenant demand might be as "risky" as they're prepared to go. For a skilled tradesperson with good local contacts, refurbishing a property and selling it on for a profit may not seem risky at all, provided the price is right and there's margin for error in the calculations. It's all a matter of perspective and what works for you personally.

5. What's your superpower?

When picking your strategy, you should think about what unique abilities you have that could unlock extra value. If you're a great negotiator, you should think about how to use that. If you're a skilled interior designer, then pick a strategy where you can use your superpower to generate supernormal profits. Carry out an audit of your skills and try to be honest with yourself about your strengths and weaknesses. Come up with a plan to work on your weaknesses and make the most of your strengths.

Common pitfalls and mistakes

There are lots of potential pitfalls and mistakes that people make when they're picking a strategy. Here are a few common ones:

- Picking something you'll hate – Sometimes, the strategy that's right from a financial perspective and that takes into account all your constraints turns out to be something you'll hate. If that's the case for you, think about how you might relax one or more of your constraints, perhaps by working to a longer timeframe or lowering your income or wealth target.

- Overestimating your resources – Whether it be free time or capital to invest, lots of new property investors overestimate their available resources. Even worse is when investors don't agree the trade-offs they're making with their partner. Good luck explaining that you can't pick little Billy up from football practice, because you decided to self-manage one of your properties and the tenant just locked themselves out of the flat.

- Not moving with the times – Property, like any other business, is constantly changing. Good areas to invest two years ago are yesterday's news; property financing strategies that once worked like a charm are no longer available. If you're going to succeed in property over the long term, you need to be clear about where you want to go, but flexible about how you get there.

Finally, it's worth a comment on celebrating your successes. Property investors (the successful ones at least) can be fairly driven types who are good at sticking to a plan and working themselves hard to achieve remarkable things. If you fall into this camp, remember to take the time to celebrate your successes every once in a while. It doesn't have to be reaching a big goal, it can be filing your first set of annual accounts or finding a tenant for your latest property. This kind of positive reinforcement can help keep you motivated over the long term and will also buy you some brownie points for that time when you leave little Billy hanging. In all seriousness, be kind to yourself and celebrate your successes.

Play # 7 – Assemble your property dream team

Linh and her partner Matt were both creative types. Linh worked for an ad agency, and Matt was a project manager for a web development company, so they knew a thing or two about good design – something they hoped to put to good use in a new side venture, refurbishing and flipping properties. They were confident about the project management and design aspects of the work; what they weren't so confident with were the legal, accounting and tax aspects of the venture. If they were going to make this successful, they'd need to get a good team around them to help.

Investing is a team sport

Being a star individual at work or in school may get you where you need to go, but it's not so in the world of investing. Investing is a team sport. The better a team player you are and the better the team around you, the higher your chances of success. There's so much to know in property that you can't possibly be an expert in everything. You need a team around you to fill out your knowledge, help ensure you're making the best possible investments, and structure your deals in the right way. Property is a people business, and it's the people you have around you that will dictate your level of success.

In this play, we're going to take a look at how to assemble your property dream team. We're going to look at what kinds of property professionals there are out there whose knowledge you can tap into. We'll look at which ones you absolutely need to have on your team versus which ones are just nice-to-haves, how to make sure you're working with the best advisors, and how to get the best out of these relationships over time. If you're time poor and have big property goals, getting the right team around you might be the single biggest thing you can do to increase your chances of success.

Building your property team

In the long run, a good professional advisor should save you more money than they charge. So, assembling a great team around you should save you both time and money. Let's look at some of the professionals you might want to have in your property team.

Solicitor

When you buy a property, you'll need a solicitor to take care of the conveyancing work. As such, a good solicitor is an essential part of your property team. You want a solicitor that's used to working with investors, not just home buyers. They need to be proactive, responsive, and on top of the detail, without being too risk-averse or taking offence at the little things that crop up. Ultimately, they need to understand you and what you're trying to achieve. If your strategy is niche or relies on speed of execution, this is even more important.

Mortgage broker

A good mortgage broker will save you time and money. Yes, they'll be able to get you the best mortgage deal – that's their job. But they will also know what type of individuals are a good fit for which lenders and which properties those lenders will and won't lend on – criteria which change all the time and are hard to keep track of yourself. You should use a whole-of-market broker that's not tied to a particular lender and one that charges a fee for their service. Paying a fee will ensure they're working for you and that your interests are aligned.

Accountant / tax advisor

Unless you're investing through a limited company, it's perfectly possible to go it alone. However, a specialist property accountant will know all the tax deductions you can claim and will work with you to optimise your tax liabilities. This is certainly an area where working with a professional will save you more money than they charge you. Ideally, you want to work with a specialist accountant or tax advisor that's also a property investor themselves. That way, you'll be able to talk to them about your long-term goals and strategy too.

Lettings agent

If you're going to outsource the day-to-day property management tasks, then you'll also need a lettings agent on your team. In fact, if you invest remotely in many different areas of the UK, you may need to partner up with a local letting agent in each area you invest. A good letting agent will make your life easier, rather than harder. They'll be able to advise you on how to secure the maximum rent, they'll find tenants quickly to minimise your void periods, and they'll be on-the-ball when it comes to the day-to-day management, saving you time.

Property sourcer

A property sourcer is an individual or a company that sources investment deals and who charges a fee for their service. You don't need a property sourcer on your team, but having one can increase the volume of deals (deal flow) crossing your desk and make it easier to hit your investment objectives. A good property sourcer should be able to secure a better deal than you can get yourself, even after taking into account their sourcing fee, so using one can accelerate your progress. This space is pretty unregulated though, so watch out for sharks. You can protect yourself by vetting the deals they bring you as you would any other investment.

Builder

If you plan on making property flips or refurbishments part of your strategy, then you're going to need a good builder on your team. Again, if you're investing across several parts of the country, you may need local contacts in each of these areas. A good builder is an extremely valuable asset in its own right, so if you find one look after them and treat them well. Be reasonable with your requests and pay them on time. Also, try to cultivate a long-term relationship where they come to see you more as a partner and less like a one-off customer.

Mentor

It's worth thinking about whether a property mentor could help you to accelerate your progress and help you achieve your goals much quicker. There are lots of different types of mentor, from an informal mentor that you check in with once in a while to a more formal paid relationship with a property coach. Because this is such an important topic, we're going to dedicate a whole section to this later in the book. If you're interested in reading more on this now, you can flick straight to play # 9, find yourself a property mentor.

Closer to home

One of the most overlooked members of your property team might actually be your life partner. Some of the most successful investors I know are couples that invest together. If your goals are aligned and if you want the same things out of life, then there's an extra strength and robustness that comes with this that you're unlikely to find anywhere else. You know each other's strengths and weakness, what you each enjoy and what you don't, and you're already financially tied in a way you'll never get with a business partner. To unlock the power of your closest relationship, you need to be open and honest about your finances, commit to some shared long-term goals, and work hard to make that relationship stable and rewarding for both of you over time.

Play # 8 – Get set up with the right tax structure

After the last financial crisis in 2007 to 2008, property prices around the UK crashed, falling up to 40% in certain locations. Frank and his wife Lucy had done well in the crash. They'd managed to snag a few bargains and build a decent sized rental portfolio on the back of the growth that came later. But they'd bought all the properties in their personal names, and the 2015 tax changes to mortgage interest relief hit them hard. By 2020, they were paying more tax than ever, and they felt a little trapped. They were thinking about investing through a limited company, but that was no quick fix either. Any restructuring of their existing portfolio would likely involve extra cost.

Getting it right

Like it or not, the amount of tax you pay will affect your final investment profits. As such, getting set up with the right tax structure is important, and starting out with the wrong structure could cost you hundreds or thousands of pounds each year in lost returns. In this section, we're going to look at the two main options most investors use to set up their portfolio, what taxes you'll pay under each, and how you can work out which structure is right for you. I'll also share some further reading and useful resources for those who want to find out more.

It's worth saying that tax is a big topic and one where things are constantly evolving. What I'll cover here is just a starting point, and it isn't a replacement for taking professional tax advice. Hopefully, it will give you a feel for what the right tax structure might be for you, and it will arm you with enough knowledge to seek out an expert that can help. The right tax structure will depend on your personal circumstances and on your goals. It's something that needs careful consideration, so make sure you take the time to get it right.

What taxes will you pay?

Whatever your property strategy, be that buy-to-lets, serviced accommodation, or holiday lets, the two main options available for setting up your property rental business are as a sole trader or as a limited company. Let's take a look at how these options work and what taxes you'll pay.

The sole trader

If you set up your business as a sole trader, you'll buy properties and let them out in your own name. The main taxes you pay will be as follows:

- Income tax – You'll pay income tax on your rental profits – that is, the profit you make after you deduct your running costs from your rental income.
- Capital gains tax – When you sell a property, you'll be taxed on the gain you make, i.e. the increase in value after allowing for all your purchase costs.

You (or your estate) could also be liable to pay inheritance tax on the value of your portfolio when you die, but that's beyond the scope of this discussion.

The income and capital gains tax rates, as well as the different thresholds and allowances, change all the time, and you can look up the latest rates on the gov.uk website. What you need to know is that the rate you pay depends on whether you're a higher or a basic rate taxpayer, with higher rate taxpayers paying more tax on income and capital gains. Also, there's currently a capital gains tax (CGT) allowance you can offset against the gain you make when you sell a property, in order to lower your tax bill. Again, details are on the gov.uk website.

The limited company

If you set your business up as a limited company, then your company will buy and let out the properties. The main taxes you'll pay will be as follows:

- Corporation tax – The company will pay corporation tax on rental profits and on any capital gain you make when you sell a property.
- Income tax – As the owner of the limited company, you'll pay income tax on any dividends you receive from the company.

The corporation tax rate changes all the time, and you can look up the latest rates on the gov.uk website. In recent years, corporation tax rates have been lower than the income tax rate for higher rate taxpayers and at a similar level to the rate for basic rate taxpayers. You should also know there's no CGT allowance for limited companies, so companies are taxed on the full gain they make when they sell a property, another difference versus owning property in your own name.

When you take money out of a company, i.e. by paying dividends to yourself as a shareholder, you will pay income tax on those dividends. Once again, higher rate taxpayers will pay more tax on dividend income than basic rate taxpayers, though there is a dividend allowance which allows you to draw some dividends out from the company tax-free. Full details of this are on the gov.uk website.

Stamp duty

When you buy a property, you'll need to pay stamp duty on the market value of the property. This is true whether you buy the property as an individual or as a limited company. However, it's worth pointing out that if you don't already own any property and you buy a property in your own name, e.g. to use as your home, you'll pay less stamp duty – you'll avoid the stamp duty surcharge that investors need to pay when they buy investment properties.

Which structure is right for you?

At this point, you might be wondering which of these structures is right for you. Although this is a complex decision, here's a look at some of the main factors you should take into account:

1. The headline tax rate

You should be aiming to pay as little tax as (legally) possible; this means picking the structure with the lowest headline rate of tax. With the corporation tax rate currently at 19% vs a 40% income tax rate for higher rate taxpayers, investing through a limited company will give higher rate taxpayers a lower headline rate. If you're a basic rate taxpayer, the headline income tax rate is currently 20%, and the comparison is not so clear cut.

2. Mortgage interest relief

Recent changes to mortgage interest tax relief mean that if you buy property in your own name, you can no longer deduct mortgage interest payments from your rental income as a cost of doing business. Instead, you get to deduct 20% of your interest cost from your final tax bill. Under this new system, higher rate taxpayers will pay more tax, and some basic rate taxpayers will also be pushed into the 40% tax bracket. None of this applies to limited companies, and interest costs are still tax deductible. Interestingly, the changes don't apply to short term holiday lets you buy in your own name, as these are classified slightly differently.

3. Potential for double taxation

If you buy property in your personal name, you only pay tax on your rental profits once. However, if you buy in a limited company, the company pays corporate tax on its profits and then you pay income tax on the dividends you take out, meaning there is a potential for double taxation. If you don't need the income to live off, you can of course leave the money in the limited company and reinvest it in future property purchases. Also, any money you inject into the company via a director's loan to get the company started or to fund property purchases can be taken out without paying tax on the withdrawal.

4. The cost of borrowing

Although interest rates have come down and the landscape has recently become more competitive, borrowing costs remain higher for limited companies than for those investing in their personal name. At the time of writing, the interest rate on a 75% loan-to-value mortgage is around 3.0% to 4.0% p.a. for a limited company and around 2.5% to 3.5% p.a. if you buy in your own name.

5. Administration costs

When you run a limited company, that comes with extra responsibilities that you don't have when you invest in your own name. You'll need to file a set of accounts each year with Companies House, and the accounts will need to be prepared in accordance with UK GAAP. You'll also need to file a CT600 corporation tax return with HMRC. As such, if you go down the limited company route, you'll need to pay an accountant to prepare these for you, so there are extra costs.

Pulling it all together

Any clearer now? Here's my take on it all. If you're just starting out in property, if you're a higher rate taxpayer, and if you plan to reinvest your profits to build a decent sized portfolio, then the limited company route might be right for you. You'll pay a lower tax rate, your mortgage interest costs will be fully deductible, and you won't get taxed twice, as you're leaving the money in the company. Also, the higher running costs won't be too onerous, if you're planning to build a larger portfolio of say five to ten properties.

If you're a basic rate taxpayer, if you only plan to buy one or two properties, and if you need the income to live off, you'll likely be better off investing in your personal name. Your tax rate will be similar under either route; however, the extra administration costs for a limited company will be high relative to the profit you're making, and the potential for double taxation will also make the company route less attractive. The fact that borrowing costs are currently cheaper in your own name makes this option more attractive too.

If your circumstances are a bit more nuanced, if you're a bit of a mix and match of the above, then it may be less clear cut. As always, you should seek some advice from a professional tax advisor or an accountant to see what's best for you in light of your personal circumstances.

What if you already own properties?

If you already own properties in your own name, you should think about what to do with these. The same considerations will apply as above, but the decision on whether to keep them in your name or transfer them to a limited company is less straightforward, as there are costs attached to a transfer like this. What you need to weigh up is how the tax savings you achieve on transferring properties to a limited company compare with the upfront costs of the transfer itself.

It is possible to transfer properties to a limited company. To do this, you need to sell the properties to the company at their current market value, which means you could be liable to pay capital gains tax. In addition, the company will have to pay stamp duty when it buys the property from you. In short, that means there are extra costs when you transfer the properties, and you need to weigh up how big these costs could be versus the tax savings you'll achieve via the transfer. This can be complicated, and it's one to take advice on, so do make sure you speak to an accountant or tax advisor if you're considering this.

If transferring properties to a company doesn't sound cost effective for you, then there may still be things you can do to get more tax efficient. You could, for example, consider transferring the ownership of part or all of your properties to your spouse or vice versa. This might be a way to "equalise" your incomes, and it can offer a tax saving, if you or your spouse is a basic rate taxpayer. Again, you should take some advice from a professional on this option, if you think it might work for you.

Further reading and useful resources

If you're looking for some specific tax advice or for a more detailed discussion on what we've covered here, you might like to check out the following resources:

- the Tax Cafe books by Carl Bayley, available on Amazon
- the Government website at gov.uk for the latest on tax rates and tax reliefs
- the tax sections of the Property Tribes and Property Hub chat forums

Finally, it's worth pointing out that in this section we've mainly covered tax issues relating to property rental businesses. If your property strategy means you'll also be flipping properties for a profit, you should think about what the right vehicle is for those projects. In general, you'll need to separate your property rental activities and property flipping activities into two separate business, as they're treated differently from a tax perspective. Again, if you're in doubt as to the best structure, make sure you get some professional advice on this.

Play # 9 – Find yourself a property mentor

Patrick had big property dreams. He wanted to grow a portfolio of HMOs targeted at young professionals and which brought in income of £4,000 per month, all in the space of three years. His main problem was that he'd never invested in property before, not even a basic buy-to-let. He figured the only way he was going to achieve this was with the help of a mentor. His plan was simple – find someone who ran HMOs for a living and ask them to teach him everything they knew. He'd pay them to mentor him, if needed.

Swimming with sharks

For many people starting out in property, the idea of finding a mentor, someone who's been where they want to go and who can help them get there, is appealing. However, whilst there's definitely benefit in working with talented investors and gaining from their experience, there's also a lot of property sharks out there who would happily take your hard-earned cash and provide little in return. In this section, we're going to look at the different types of relationship you could enter into with a potential mentor, when it makes sense to pay for coaching and advice, and some of the keys to success in choosing a property mentor.

Three types of property mentor

Before we get into the detail here, it's worth checking that you do need a mentor and not something else instead. Have a look at the following questions:

- Are you searching for property information or general motivation?
- Are you seeking out a companion to share in your property journey?
- Are you looking for a way to "go public" to hold yourself accountable?

If the answer to any of these questions is yes, then you might be better off meeting these needs in other ways, i.e. you might not need a property mentor.

For example, you can get lots of property information and motivation from reading books and blogs, joining property forums, and listening to some of the great free podcasts out there. Likewise, getting face time with other investors and expanding your network through networking events can be a great way to find like-minded people and partner up with someone for accountability.

With all of that said, let's look at three different types of property mentor you could develop to help you fast-track your property progress.

The trusted advisor

If you've followed the advice of play # 7 and assembled a great team around you, then you'll likely already be getting mentoring for free. The professional advisors you have in your property team will have all kinds of knowledge and expertise you can make use of everyday and they'll be happy to share it. The best advisors love to talk about what they do, and they'll be keen to give you advice. You just have to pick great people to work with.

The annual one-hour review meeting I have with my own accountant is one of the most valuable hours of my year. Whilst the session is there principally to run through my accounting figures and reporting, it always turns into a much wider conversation about my strategy and my next steps. Being an investor himself, his advice is excellent, and more than once he's challenged my logic and pushed my buttons in a way that's helped me to make better decisions.

The informal mentor

Property is one of those walks of life where people love to share their knowledge. If you've ever been to a property networking event, one of the good ones anyway, then you've probably been surprised and overwhelmed by the number of people that are happy to share what they do and help newcomers to the field. Yes, you'll meet some unscrupulous types who are just looking to sell something, but you'll also meet a whole host of great people that you can build relationships with and that you can leverage to help you progress.

This kind of informal mentoring tends to work best when it happens naturally. For example, if you meet someone who's already doing what you want to do, be that buy-to-lets or flips, and they're a little bit further along in their journey, why not ask them to swap contact details and see if they'd be open to checking in once in a while for a property chat. If you ask them to be your mentor or try to define the relationship too formally, then you might scare them off.

The property coach

In general, my advice is to stay clear of anyone calling themselves a property coach or who's selling a coaching service. That's not the same thing as saying you should never pay for a coach, just that you're unlikely to get value from someone who's putting themselves out there as one. In my experience, the best coaches get most of their work through referrals, so the way to find a good coach is through a recommendation from a fellow investor.

Paying for a coach to help you achieve better or faster results is a perfectly reasonable thing to do, but you need to make sure you're getting value for money. If a paid mentor can give you access to systems and experience that accelerates your progress and pays you back handsomely through better returns, or if having their opinion on potential deals can help prevent you making expensive mistakes, then it might be worth paying for a coach. But don't rush in – see what you can get for free and only pay for what you have to.

Keys to success

If you're going to make use of a property mentor, whether that be an informal mentor or a paid coach, there are some important things you should do to make sure the relationship works and that you get the advice you need.

- Pick someone who's done what you want to do – Mentoring works best when you want to learn something specific, like how to run a successful HMO. Pick someone who's exactly where you want to be, not just successful in general.

- Get in the goldilocks zone – If the gap in experience is too big, you're likely to find the advice too high-level or out-of-date. If the person is only a little bit ahead of you in their own journey, they might have less to offer.

- Avoid authority figures and property gurus – It goes without saying, but you should avoid gurus or anyone marketing themselves as an authority. Also, avoid full-time property coaches – the best mentors are active in their field.

- Avoid expensive coaching and upfront payments – If you're going to pay for coaching, make sure it's not too expensive and arrange it so that you pay for each session as you go. That way, you can cancel if it's not working out.

- Go with your gut feel – Listen to your subconscious and go with your gut feel. If your spidey-senses are tingling and telling you something's wrong, or if you don't think the relationship will be a good fit, then just politely decline.

Finally, the main test I use when deciding who I want to work with is the listening test. In short, you should try to work with someone who listens to you and wants to understand what you're trying to achieve. You can gauge this by the quality of the questions they ask or by whether they ask any questions at all. If they're just trying to sell you something, it won't be long before they turn the conversation round to themselves and what they have to offer you.

Part Two : Gathering your resources

Play # 10 – Get a second job or start a side hustle

However hard he tried, Daniel just couldn't meet his savings target of £2,000 per month. He'd cut down on the take-aways and nights out, cancelled his Netflix subscription, and switched his mobile contract to a sim-only deal – but he was still averaging just £1,500 per month. That's when he decided to put his skills as a maths teacher to good use. Over the next three months, by signing up to a number of online tutoring websites, Daniel built a part-time tutoring business that brought in an extra £400 to £500 a month. The three to four hours he gave up each Saturday to tutor students not only helped him meet his savings target, they also made him a better teacher too.

A bit on the side

At the start of their property journey, the biggest constraint most people face is a lack of funds. Even with all the will in the world, the right education, and a strong team in place, you won't get very far without a decent capital base. It's for this reason that many budding investors look for ways to increase their income through a second job or a side hustle. In this section, we'll take a look at some of the most common ways to generate an extra income outside of the day job, the challenges this can bring, and some common pitfalls and mistakes.

Moonlighting for extra income

Moonlighting refers to the practice of having a second job, typically held secretly at night, in addition to one's regular employment. To avoid conflicts with their main job, moonlighters often opt for simple jobs that can be done in the hours outside their regular job, e.g. at weekends, or jobs that are more flexible in nature. Let's take a look at some examples.

Types of second job

- Evening and weekend jobs – There are a variety of evening and weekend jobs available to the moonlighter. Everything from late night petrol station clerk and waiting tables at a nearby restaurant to early morning shifts at your local supermarket on Saturday mornings.

- Work the gig economy – Apps like Deliveroo and Uber have made flexible side gigs available to anyone with some mode of transport and the grit and determination to put themselves out there. Although they don't pay well, the flexibility of the work does have an appeal for many.

- Work your existing skillset – Targeting a job that uses your existing skillset can offer the prospect of a better hourly rate. If you teach maths in the day job, why not try teaching an evening class at your local college. If you're an accountant, take on some bookkeeping work at the weekends.

- Overtime and extra shifts – Although not technically a second job, many jobs do offer the potential for overtime and extra shifts. Ask your employer what extra roles and responsibilities you could take on for additional income and you might be surprised at the results.

- Seasonal work – At certain times of the year, seasonal work opportunities abound. At Christmas, you might find a weekend job selling Christmas trees. In the summer, there are often temporary jobs in farming and tourism. As the saying goes, make hay while the sun shines.

Keys to success

Although moonlighting can be a great way to earn some extra income and speed up your investment progress, it's not without its challenges. At the heart of this strategy is a simple time-for-money trade-off, which may not work for everyone, particular those in inflexible or time-demanding day jobs.

The key to success here lies in being realistic about what's possible, given the wider constraints on your time. Although you may love the idea of earning an extra £500 to £1,000 per month working weekends at your local supermarket (you glutton for punishment you) that might not be feasible if you have childcare responsibilities or family commitments. Likewise, if your day job is demanding and requires the full attention of an alert and skilful mind, there's no point tiring yourself out on the late shift at your local watering hole. Property investment should be a long-term endeavour, so try to apply a long-term mindset to these kinds of decisions. If you're in doubt about whether you can make this work, try doing just a little bit first and scale up from there.

I also have one final word of warning on this topic. Many salaried jobs in the UK incorporate a "no moonlighting clause" into their employment contracts. This type of clause typically prohibits the employee taking on a second job without the approval of their employer. If you're in this position, you should think carefully about your options. If the second job presents no obvious conflicts of interest, i.e. if it's in a different industry or sector to your main job, your employer's concerns will likely be limited to whether you're taking on too much and whether the second job will interfere with your current duties. If the second job is in a similar industry, it might get a little more complicated. Even if your employment contract has no such clause and doesn't require you disclose this kind of information, it's usually always better to be open and honest with your employer about your plans. If you handle this badly and your employer takes a dim view of your choices, you could face a much greater set back in reaching your property goals. Again, it's important to apply a long-term mindset.

The tao of the side hustle

If taking on a second job doesn't sound like much fun (who wants another boss, right?) then an alternative path to creating some additional income is to start a side hustle. Although the precise meaning of the term is still in flux, a side hustle is generally taken to mean starting some kind of business, rather than simply getting a second job. That is, a side hustle is a small business you run for yourself on your own terms. You work for yourself, not for your employer, and you decide how much time and energy you want to devote to it. Think of it as something akin to being a part-time entrepreneur.

There are many different types of side hustle. If you decide to go down this route, you should pick something that both motivates you and that you have the skills and expertise to pull off. Starting a business from scratch is hard, and you don't want to make it harder for yourself by picking something that's ill-suited to you and your background. With that in mind, let's take a look at some common side hustles and the kind of skills and expertise you need to make them a success. Hopefully at least one of the items below will be something that appeals to you and that you think you could have a go at.

Types of side hustle

- Start an online business – If you're tech-savvy, then why not start an online business. Lots of people make good money selling products on stores like Amazon, eBay, and Etsy. Or you could think about starting up a website and selling your products through Shopify instead.
- Launch a sweaty start-up – Sweaty start-ups are small, local businesses, e.g. window cleaning, power-washing drives and patios, removal companies, etc. Ideally, the business you choose should be low cost to start, i.e. it shouldn't require a lot of expensive equipment, and be do-able in your free time.
- Offer a productised service – If you come from a professional background, the natural business to start would be one that uses your skillset. If you work

in finance, start a small bookkeeping business; if you're a graphic designer, launch your own graphic design agency.

- Turn a hobby into gold – Many people have hobbies they could easily turn into a side hustle. If magic is your hobby, become a close-up magician for hire at weddings and birthday parties; if you're a great musician, why not start a band and hire yourself out to corporate events.

- Become a freelancer – Starting your own freelancing business is a great side hustle. Websites like Upwork and Bark allow you to market your skills and pitch for freelance jobs posted by potential clients. Whatever your skillset, there's likely to be someone who's looking to buy at a reasonable price.

Keys to success

Starting a business, even a small side hustle, can be extremely demanding and time consuming. Entrepreneurship is a skillset in its own right, and working long hours for relatively modest returns to get a new business off the ground is not for everyone. Those of you who see property investment as a fascinating challenge and part of a longer-term personal journey may view starting a business in the same way – as a great adventure that's worthwhile in its own right. If that sounds like you, starting a side hustle might be right up your street.

Again, the key to success here is being realistic about what's possible given the wider constraints on your time. You should pick a business that interests you and that you have the skills, expertise and resources to carry out. Remember, it's not about designing an app, inventing some new gadget, or coming up with a new business idea or concept – it's about finding a market where people are already spending money and getting your product or service out there quickly to see if you can make some money. Calling at houses in your local area that have dirty driveways and asking if you can power-wash their drive for £250 is not rocket science, but it is good business and it can make you some extra money on the side. These are the kinds of side hustle you should be looking to start.

A final word on tax

If you do secure a second job or start a side business, you'll need to make sure you're tax compliant. If this is the first time you've ventured outside the PAYE system, you'll need to get up-to-speed on the relevant tax requirements, in light of your personal circumstances and the type of business you've started. If you're setting up as a sole trader, you'll need to register with HMRC for self-assessment; if you're setting up as a limited company, you'll need help from an accountant filing year end financial statements and a corporation tax return. Don't let these aspects put you off, but do take them seriously and educate yourself to make sure you're 100% comfortable with the requirements. Also, get the right team in place to help you out with this.

Reversal

There are times when getting a second job or starting a side business is not the quickest path to extra income. Sometimes your main job is the easiest route to earning more, for example, by taking on extra responsibility, striving for another promotion, or working hard for a larger bonus. If you're already highly valued by your employer, this might even be as simple as asking for a raise or expressing your interest in taking on more responsibility.

You could consider developing a specialist skillset or getting into a particular product or service niche, if this would enhance your prospects of promotion. You might also consider completing additional qualifications or retraining, if these paths could unlock your earnings potential. The thing to keep in mind at all times here is the time versus money trade-off – you want to maximise both your total earnings and hourly rate and getting this balance right is key to your success over the long term.

Play # 11 – Consider a radical baselining

Bailey spent hours on Rightmove, but he couldn't find anything that looked even vaguely reasonable – everything was either too pricey or looked like the inside of a shoebox. Living in London was going to be more expensive than he'd imagined. After speaking with his parents, he had a brainwave. Rather than fork out £700 per month to live in shared accommodation, he'd call his uncle and see if he could board with him for a while, until he settled into his new role. His uncle was happy to accommodate him, and the arrangement helped Bailey cut his monthly expenses in half.

What's it all about?

In the previous section, we considered a number of ways new investors might go about generating some extra cash to invest. In this play, we're going to focus on the other side of the coin – that is, we're going to look at how we might radically cut down our monthly living expenses instead. The net result is the same, i.e. an increased level of savings to kick start our property journey, but it's often easier to cut down your expenses than it is to generate additional income, so it can lead to some quick and easy wins.

At the heart of this play is a concept known as *baselining*. This term, which originates from the world of budgeting, generally refers to the idea of moving to a lower cost location or cutting your living expenses dramatically by some other means, with the aim of freeing up resources to use in other endeavours. If you're a budding entrepreneur, this could be with the aim of getting your business off the ground; for property investors, this might be to increase your savings rate and build your portfolio faster. To quote Dave Ramsey, the personal finance guru, the idea is to "live like no one else, so you can live like no one else".

Baselining strategies

At its core, baselining requires some kind of radical change in your way of living. There are many ways to achieve this, and some will be easier than others given your personal circumstances and your existing work commitments. All of them, however, will likely involve some kind of personal sacrifice – after all, sometimes it's necessary to do a little bad in order to achieve a much greater good. Let's take a look at some common baselining strategies.

Take advantage of geographic arbitrage

Geographic arbitrage means taking advantage of the difference in costs between two geographic locations. The lighter touch version of this strategy could mean, for example, moving ten miles up the road to lower your rental costs. The more extreme version could mean asking your boss if you can relocate, perhaps to an office in a cheaper city somewhere else in the country.

In the UK, it's generally cheaper to live outside a city centre than inside, and it's generally cheaper to live in the north than the south. Beware of any knock-on impacts of the potential move though, as moving further outside the hustle and bustle can lead to increased travel costs. You'll need to weigh up all of these factors and come up with a view on what's the best solution in the round, perhaps factoring in any increase in your travel time too.

Downsizing and downshifting

No, I'm not talking about the ridiculous 2017 movie starring Matt Damon, but I am talking about reducing the amount of space you need (or think you need) and the amount of superfluous stuff in your life. At the heart of these strategies is a shift towards minimalism and away from the natural human tendency to want more stuff and keep up with the Joneses.

Downsizing is when you move into smaller, less expensive accommodation. It can be a great way to lower your costs. Ask yourself what's the minimum space you could reasonably handle. For a young family, this might be a two-bedroom house; for a couple, a one-bedroom apartment. If you're single, this might mean living with friends or in shared accommodation. Downshifting is when you try to simplify your lifestyle, consume less, and escape the "work-and-spend cycle" that many people are so caught up in. Both of these areas are ripe for experimentation and should form part of your overall baselining strategy.

Negotiate a remote working arrangement

Fancy eliminating your travel costs entirely or cutting your cost of living by 50%? Then a remote working arrangement might be for you. In the modern working world, there are lots of jobs that can be performed anywhere you have a half-decent internet connection and a laptop. This opens up the possibility for even more aggressive baselining, like having a job in one country and living in another, where the costs of living might be even lower.

For example, you could work from Lisbon in Portugal, where a two-bedroom apartment rents for just £500 per month and where monthly groceries for two people might cost £600. If this is a possibility with your line of work, why not try a conversation with your employer and see what they say. Many companies are just waking up to the possibilities that remote working arrangements create, so why not help them out a little and see if you can negotiate a win-win for you and your employer.

Move in with someone else

At the more extreme end of the baselining spectrum, you could consider moving back home with your parents, moving in with a friend, or perhaps moving in with a romantic partner. I listened to a podcast recently where Robert Kiyosaki of Rich Dad Poor Dad fame talked about some of the personal sacrifices he and his wife, Kim, had made when they were first starting out. One of these was to live in the basement of a friend's house for over a year to cut their living costs while they tried to get a new business off the ground. Which just goes to show that it's not always obvious what sacrifices people have made to achieve success.

This particular baselining strategy is definitely easier if you're single and if you don't have children or caring responsibilities. In London, where rents are amongst the highest in the UK, I see this strategy used by new graduates all the time. If your parents live close by and if they're happy to have you around, why not move back in with them for a while. Yes, it might restrict your social life a bit, but think about how much extra you could save and the years it could shave off your investment goals. It's not a strategy to be sniffed at, and it can make a real difference, particularly if you stick with it for a number of years.

Live a fully mobile lifestyle

Finally, you could even consider doing without a permanent home altogether and living a fully mobile lifestyle. There are people who choose to live in motorhomes that live a great life on the road rent-free; others choose to live on riverboats and barges. And they're not all give-peace-a-chance hippy types. There are plenty of stories about software engineers sacking off their overpriced apartments in San Francisco and basing themselves out of trucks on the Google campus. This really is at the extreme end of what's possible with baselining, but it's all about personal choice, and if this is something you think you'll enjoy, then why not give it a try for yourself.

Limitations of baselining

The idea of baselining does have its attractions. For one, there's something in the concept that speaks to the inner rebel – the chance to stick it to the man and beat the system somehow. What's more, the Government can't tax a saving in the same way they can tax extra income, meaning you'll get to keep every pound you save without having to declare it on your tax return.

But there's a limit to how far you can push things without adversely impacting one or more of your health, your relationships, your work and job prospects, and your happiness. If you've got to the point where your girlfriend or boyfriend is threatening to move out because they don't like the idea of living in a car park, or if your friends have stopped answering your calls because trying to save money on soap has impacted your personal hygiene, then you know you've pushed it too far. It's really all about balance.

As a final caveat, you should make sure to think about how your baselining strategy will impact on your ability to borrow. Those of no fixed abode generally have a harder time convincing the banks to lend to them, which may hamper your ability to invest. Likewise, if you're considering spending a large part of your year working and living abroad, you should make sure you fully understand the tax implications. This can affect your UK residence status and impact how and where you need to pay taxes, in addition to limiting you financing options. If you fall into this camp, make sure you speak to a specialist tax accountant who can help you work out whether this strategy might be for you.

Play # 12 – Saving for your first investment

The hardest part about putting his plans into action was that it made him feel like an outsider. George was unusually motivated for a 23 year old, but turning down those weekly team building nights out (aka boozing sessions) with his colleagues twice a week still made him feel like a bit of loner, even if all that saving was for a good cause. Eighteen months into his journey, his effort finally paid off, when he was able to use his savings to secure his first buy-to-let investment. The property netted him a cool £250 per month in cash flow and gave him the resolve he needed to endure the next eighteen months in the cold.

The long and winding road

It might not be the sexist of topics, but saving up for your first investment is the most important thing you can do to get started. It's important because the quicker you make it happen, the quicker you start to feel the benefits of compounding – that is, the quicker the "snowball effect" kicks in and the faster you can start to build real wealth through property.

In this play, we're going to take a look at how to calculate the amount you'll need to save for your first investment, where to stash your cash while you're waiting to invest, and at some of the Government schemes you might be able to take advantage of along the way to speed up your progress. Using some simple calculations, I'll also show you how the snowball effect can start to do some of the hard work for you over time, as your portfolio grows in size.

Calculating your savings target

How much you need to save for your first investment will depend where you're planning to invest and what kind of property you want to buy. If you're planning to invest in a northern powerhouse city like Manchester, Liverpool or Leeds, you'll need less cash than if you plan to invest further south. Also, you'll need to put less money down if you're planning to buy a one-bedroom apartment, rather than a three-bedroom family house.

Let's take a simple example and walk through how to calculate the amount you'll need. I'm going to assume we're aiming to buy a two-bedroom apartment for £160,000 somewhere in the north, my usual hunting ground.

- The deposit – For a simple buy-to-let investment, you'll need to put down a deposit of at least 25% of the purchase price. This means you'll need to save at least £40,000 to cover the deposit.
- Stamp duty land tax – As an investor subject to the stamp duty surcharge, you'll need to pay stamp duty of £5,500 on a residential property purchase worth £160,000, not taking into account the temporary increase in the stamp duty threshold that will apply until 1 April 2021.
- Furnishing and redecoration – If you plan to do any redecoration after you buy the property, you'll need to pay for these costs upfront. Let's assume we'll spend £2,000 on redecoration (new flooring, a new washing machine, some painting work) and £1,500 on furnishing the apartment.
- Legal and other fees – Legal fees could be up to £2,000, including the cost of independent legal advice on personal guarantees, if you're investing through a limited company. In addition, the mortgage valuation fee might be £500, and the cost of a mortgage broker could be £500.

Based on the above, you'd need to save around £52,000 to do this deal and make sure you had sufficient funds left to get the property into the right condition to let out. You can adapt these workings as needed to set your own savings target, based on the areas you're looking to invest and the kind of properties you're planning to buy. Remember to make sure you're working from the latest stamp duty rates and thresholds – you can find these on the gov.uk website – and make sure you build in the 3% surcharge for second homes.

Where to invest your funds

Depending on your target, it could take a while, possibly a number of years, to build up enough funds for your first deal. While you're waiting, keep your savings somewhere safe, and, if you can try, to generate some extra return by investing them. This will lower the amount you need to save to meet your target, and it will help you get there a bit quicker. Let's take a look at some key considerations when choosing where to park your monies.

Time horizon

Your investment time horizon is likely to be fairly short. That is, you'll probably want to withdraw your funds in a couple of years' time at the point where you're ready to invest. In practice, therefore, you won't want to keep your savings locked away for periods longer than one or two years. So, this will rule out longer term, higher rate savings accounts that keep your money tied up for two years or more. It will also rule out a variety of long-term bonds, e.g. five or ten-year Government and corporate bonds.

Volatility

Because your investment time horizon is short, you should avoid asset classes that are too volatile. In practice, this means you should avoid the stock market, cryptocurrencies like Bitcoin, and investments where the volatility is typically in excess of 15% to 20% per annum. Afterall, you don't want to save hard for two years to build a deposit of £50,000 only to have the stock market crash and the value of your savings fall to £30,000. Falls of this magnitude are possible in the stock market at times of market turmoil and stress, and you should make sure you're not exposed to this risk.

Tax efficiency

Finally, you should also look for savings options that are tax efficient. In the UK, you might, depending on your circumstances, need to pay tax on savings interest. You can check out the gov.uk website for full details on the various rules and allowances that cover tax on savings. In practice, it's often simpler and easier to stick with one of the tax-exempt savings vehicles, such as cash ISAs (Individual Savings Accounts) or Premium Bonds, offered by NS&I. The prizes on Premium Bonds are tax-free and the effective interest rate is better than you'd get in most bank accounts right now.

Schemes to help you out

It's also worth thinking about whether there are any Government schemes you could take advantage of to speed up your progress. Although you won't be able to use them to invest in buy-to-let properties or to carry out that next flip, these schemes might help if buying (play # 13), refurbishing (play # 16) or extending (play # 19) your own home forms part of your overall strategy. Here's a summary of two Government schemes on offer at the time of writing.

- The Lifetime ISA – You can use a Lifetime ISA to buy your first home or save for later life. The general idea is that you can put in up to £4,000 each year and the Government will add a 25% bonus to your savings, up to a maximum of £1,000 per year. You can withdraw your money and use it to buy your first home, provided that the property costs £450,000 or less.
- Help to Buy Equity Loan – With the Help to Buy Equity Loan, you can get a low interest loan from the Government to put towards a deposit. The home

must be a new build available through one of the Help to Buy Agents and be the only property you own. Also, you can't sublet it or rent it out. The price must be less than £600,000 in England (or £300,000 in Wales). You need to put in a 5% deposit, the Government will lend you up to 20% to top up your deposit, and the rest you'll buy with a mortgage. You pay no interest on the Government loan for the first five years; after that, you'll be charged a fee of 1.75% p.a. of the loan value. You'll need to pay back the loan when you sell the property and the amount you pay back will be scaled up or down in line with the increase or decrease in the market value of the property.

These kinds of schemes change all the time, so you should make sure to check out what's available to you at the time you're picking your own strategy. Check out the gov.uk website for the latest detail on all these schemes.

Also, don't fall into the trap of letting the tail wag the dog – that is, don't let your whole strategy be determined by one particular scheme. If you find yourself trying to twist your plans and tactics just to make use of a particular Government scheme, then it might not be right for you in the long run anyway.

The snowball effect

Getting started in property is hard. It takes a special kind of determination and belief to stick with it over the long term, setting aside savings month after month, year after year, with an uncertain future payoff. But for those who stick with it, the rewards can be handsome, and at some point the snowball effect will start to help you out along the way.

To illustrate how this concept works, let's take a look at the length of time it could take for us to save for each extra property we're planning to purchase. There's no fancy mathematics here, and we're not employing any of the strategies in this book that might speed up your journey. We're simply taking a look at how long it would take us to grow a portfolio of 20 properties through the brute force approach, i.e. via raw savings power only.

Suppose we're aiming to buy several properties around the £160,000 mark. As per our example above, we'll need to save around £50,000 for each deal. In addition, let's assumes that we're capable of saving around £2,000 per month or £24,000 per year. This means it will take us £50,000 ÷ £24,000 = 2.1 years to save for our first deal. However, if we achieve an ROI of 6% p.a. on our cash, then our first property will generate £50,000 × 0.06 = £3,000 per annum or £250 per month of additional cash flow, which will help us save for our next property deal more quickly. In the table below, I've set out how long it will take us to save for each property in our portfolio using this approach.

Property	Annual savings	Time taken to save
1	£24,000	2.1 years
2	£27,000	1.9 years
3	£30,000	1.7 years
4	£33,000	1.5 years
5	£36,000	1.4 years
6	£39,000	1.3 years
7	£42,000	1.2 years
8	£45,000	1.1 years
9	£48,000	1.0 years
10	£51,000	1.0 years
11	£54,000	0.9 years
12	£57,000	0.9 years
13	£60,000	0.8 years
14	£63,000	0.8 years
15	£66,000	0.8 years
16	£69,000	0.7 years
17	£72,000	0.7 years
18	£75,000	0.7 years
19	£78,000	0.6 years
20	£81,000	0.6 years

From the table, you can see that it will take us 8.6 years to save for our first five properties, 5.6 years to save for our next five properties, 4.2 years for the next five, and 3.3 years for the last five. That's the power of compounding and the snowball effect kicking in over time. So, even if you started your property journey at 45 years old, you could still grow a portfolio of 20 properties bringing in £5,000 per month by the time you retire. With the help of some capital growth along the way, you might even be able to do a lot better than this.

That brings us to the end of this aside on the snowball effect. I've included it here in the middle of this play on saving to keep you motivated and encourage you to stick with it over the long term. If you get disheartened or need a positive reminder of why you're doing all this, I hope you'll re-read this section on the snowball effect and that it will help you see the light at the end of the tunnel.

Further reading and useful resources

If you're looking for some specific advice on saving, you might like to check out the following websites:

- moneysavingexpert.com for savings tips on many different topics
- moneystepper.com for tips on saving and investing
- mrmoneymustache.com for some radical views on cutting expenses

If you're interested in the Government's Help to Buy schemes, then check out the gov.uk website for the latest information.

Play # 13 – Buy a home with an investment case

When Harry moved to Manchester to take a new job, the move presented him with a dilemma. Rental yields in Manchester were attractive, making the city a great place to invest; at the same time, he'd always wanted to own his own home. Harry wanted his hard-earned savings to work equally hard for him, but he also wanted a place to call his own. To eat his cake and still have it, Harry decided to buy a home with an investment case. For Harry, this option gave him the best of both worlds.

Why buy a home, rather than invest?

Having committed to property investment as a path to financial freedom, it might sound counterintuitive to buy a home, rather than choosing to invest. However, buying your own home first offers a range of advantages to the new investor, and it can be a great first step – provided it's done in the right way. The trick here is to make sure that the property you choose works as a home and stacks up as a potential buy-to-let investment, should you choose to let it out later.

Buying your own home is a great way to get started. It helps you build up your track record as a property owner. It also helps you build up a history of regular mortgage repayments each month, improving your credit score and increasing your attractiveness to lenders when you do come to invest. It can also help you get started sooner. A typical minimum deposit on a buy-to-let investment would (at the time of writing) be 25% of the purchase price; however, you might be able to purchase your own home with just a 10% deposit, meaning you can get started much sooner, albeit this mortgage will likely need to be a repayment mortgage at this sort of deposit level.

When it comes to the softer skills, buying your own home first also gives you a chance to build up your knowledge and experience of the purchasing process, and it gives you a chance to practice your deal negotiation skills in a relatively safe, low-risk environment. That is, it's a chance to try things out without feeling the full pressure of the deal on your first purchase.

So, with all of that said, when is this play the right route for a property investor to take, and how do you go about building the investment case that underpins this strategy? We'll take a closer look at this side of things now.

Building the investment case

For this strategy to be right, there are two key criteria that need to be met. Both of these elements need to be present to provide a compelling investment case:

1. the property should work as an investment in its own right; and
2. the deal should have a positive impact on your monthly cash flow

Let's take a look at each of these criteria in turn and use some numerical examples to flesh out what a compelling investment case might look like.

The property should work as an investment

In order to meet the first criteria, you'll need to find a property that's right in the sweet spot. It needs to work as a home and as a buy-to-let investment, so you'll likely be restricted to one and two-bedroom apartments and two and three-bedroom houses. Anything larger than this probably won't work from a numbers perspective, unless you've got plans to convert it into a HMO later – that's a whole different strategy we'll return to much later. In addition, this will likely rule out expensive, high-end properties such as penthouse apartments or large, detached houses where the yields just aren't attractive.

When you're weighing up the purchase from an investment perspective, you should do this on a *look-through* basis. That is, if you bought the property and immediately let it out on day-one, rather than moving in yourself, what would the property generate in terms of rental income and monthly cash flow. You should apply the same investment criteria, i.e. target capitalisation rate and return on investment, that you would use on any other property investment. If the expected return doesn't cut the mustard, then rule it out and look for something better. Remember, you're not looking for your "forever home" here; you're looking for a solid, buy-to-let property that you would be happy to live in yourself, at least for a few years while you get started.

It should positively impact your monthly cash flow

To understand whether the property meets our second criteria, we'll need to do some maths. Suppose, for example, you're considering buying a two-bedroom apartment in Leeds. You can compare the cost of renting the apartment with the cost of buying it, as per the following table.

Scenario	Renting	Buying
Purchase price	N/A	£160,000
Loan-to-value	N/A	75%
Interest rate	N/A	2.0% p.a.
Mortgage	N/A	Repayment / 25 years
Rent	£900	-
Mortgage cost	-	£509
Service charge	-	£125
Ground rent	-	£30
Maintenance	-	£50
Total monthly cost	£900	£714

In this example, the cost of renting the apartment is £900 per month. This cost is all-in, as the landlord would cover the service charge, ground rent, and repair and maintenance costs. However, if we chose to buy instead of rent, the cost of living in exactly the same apartment could be much lower. That is, our total cost could be £714 per month, if we use a repayment mortgage with a loan-to-value (LTV) of 75%. Buying therefore gives us a cash saving of £186 per month when compared with renting, and we can plough this saving back into future property investments.

Pros and cons

If the property you buy meets both of the criteria set out above, then there really aren't too many cons to this strategy. The main disadvantage in buying any home is that you're tying yourself to a particular location, but we've covered off this risk by making sure the property also works as a buy-to-let, if we suddenly need to move out and change our location, say for work reasons.

There are a couple of potential extra pros to consider here too. In the UK, there is generally no capital gains tax to pay when you sell your main residence. So, if there's an increase in the price between when you buy and when you sell, there will likely be a tax saving, if the property remains your main home for all or some of the period you own it. In addition, the lower deposit amount required, e.g. a 10% deposit versus the 25% normally required for buy-to-let, can (through the extra leverage it gives you) amplify your returns when prices are rising.

Common pitfalls and mistakes

The main pitfalls and mistakes that can arise with this strategy are when people forget to treat the purchase as an investment. Here are a few common ones:

- Paying too much – If you pay too much, this will negatively impact your returns and cash savings. This mistake is easier to make when buying your own home, as the decision can be more emotional.

- Ignoring rental demand – You need to make sure there's strong demand if you decide to let the property out in the future. Ignore rental demand in the area at your own peril.

- Furnishing and redecoration – You need to do this in a way that's suitable for the end rental market. Don't buy expensive furniture and avoid redecoration that won't be to everyone's taste.

- The exit strategy – If you do plan to move out and let out the property, you'll likely need to switch to a buy-to-let mortgage. If you've used a 10% deposit, you may need to put down an extra 15% in order to remortgage.

By far the biggest mistake people tend to make with this strategy is in their choice of property, either by buying too large a property or by investing in an area where the numbers just really don't stack up as a buy-to-let investment.

The reversal

So, when is this strategy not a good one to follow? Well, if the expected returns on buy-to-let properties in the area you want to live are not that attractive, this is probably not the right play for you. Likewise, if renting is less expensive than buying, even marginally so, this makes the case for this particular strategy much less compelling. This is the situation for most of London and the South East of England at the time of writing. In this scenario, you're probably better off renting and using your hard-earned savings to invest in an area with more attractive rental yields. Keep this under review over time though, as property prices and rental yields change throughout the property cycle, meaning even if this play doesn't work for you right now, it may well do so in the future.

Play # 14 – Earn extra cash letting out a spare room

Julia, a 33-year-old accountant, owns a three-bedroom house just outside of Nottingham. As a trainee accountant, she'd saved hard and got herself on to the property ladder, then traded her way up to a three-bedroom house. But it was a bit too much space for her. One of the rooms had been left unused and unloved, gathering dust since the day she bought it. She decided to put it to good use. Julia now lets out her spare room for around £500 a month, and the extra income pays around half of her monthly mortgage. She also likes having some company around.

What's the big idea

There's nothing complicated at all about play # 14 – this strategy is as simple as they come. Letting out a spare room can be a great way to generate some extra income each month to help you achieve that monthly savings target and reach your wider property goals faster. You might even make some friends (or at the least some interesting acquaintances) along the way. But like any other strategy, you'll need to execute this one the right way to make it a success.

At the time of writing, there's a specific UK Government scheme that provides an extra incentive for going down this route. The Rent a Room Scheme has been in place since 1992, and it currently lets you earn up to £7,500 per year tax-free from letting out furnished accommodation in your own home. You can let out as much of your home as you want; you can even opt into the scheme if you run a bed and breakfast or a guest house. To be eligible, you need to be a resident landlord, meaning you'll need to be living in the property yourself. In addition, you can't use the scheme for homes that have been converted into separate, self-contained flats – it really does have to be a room in your own home.

Keys to success

Don't be fooled by the informality of the idea itself. Giving up a room in your home to a stranger is no small ask, and it needs to be done carefully and thoughtfully. To get this strategy right, you'll need to treat this endeavour as a mini business in its own right. Importantly, you'll need a strategy and a system in place for dealing with each of the following elements:

1. finding and attracting potential lodgers
2. collecting rent and paying your bills and taxes
3. handling the legal aspects of the tenancy

Let's take a closer look at each of these three areas in turn and the kinds of things you can do to professionalise your approach and set things up the right way.

Finding and attracting potential lodgers

In today's world, there are many different ways to go about finding a potential lodger. You could, for example, go straight to your local letting agent and they'd be able to help you advertise the property, find a lodger, arrange viewings, and take care of all the legal and compliance aspects of the tenancy. This is likely to be the most expensive way to complete the task, but it's a great option if you're time poor and if you're prepared to pay a few hundred pounds for a letting agent to handle this for you.

Whether it's due to their thriftiness, masochistic tendencies, or the intimate nature of taking in a lodger, most live-in landlords prefer to go down the do-it-yourself route. That's where the internet comes in useful. The UK's busiest and most popular house-share website is spareroom.co.uk, which lets you post an advert for free. You could also opt for a service like that offered by openrent.co.uk, which lets you advertise your property directly on portals like Rightmove and Zoopla at a relatively low cost. Alternatively, if you have strong ties to the local community, e.g. through a church, student union, or a local employer, you could consider posting an advert on a community nottceboard. I've heard stories of students and young professionals having great success with this strategy, so it's not one to be overlooked. It can be an effective, low-cost way to market a property and can get you some great results.

It's a good idea to draw up a profile of your ideal lodger before you start to advertise the property. The last thing you want is to end up living with a person or a situation that makes you uncomfortable, so it can help to get clear on this from the get-go. You should think about your preferences around their gender, age and employment, whether you are prepared to accept smokers and pets, and how long a rental period you want to offer, e.g. three months, one year, indefinite. Your property or its location might also make it more suited to a particular type of lodger, e.g. students if you live near to a university or young professionals if you live close to a city centre.

Rent, bills, and income tax

You should set the rent based on the typical market rent for similar properties in the local area and you should agree it with your lodger. As a resident landlord, you will be responsible for paying the council tax and utility bills for the entire property, but you can include a charge for these within the headline rent. Also, do remember to tell your local council, if taking in a lodger means you're no longer entitled to a single person discount on your council tax.

On the income tax side, the Government's Rent a Room Scheme allows you to earn up to £7,500 per year (around £625 per month) tax-free letting out a room or part of your main residence. It must be furnished, i.e. unfurnished rooms don't qualify, and the tax exemption is automatic provided you earn less than £7,500. If you do earn more than this, you must complete a self-assessment tax return; you can then choose to pay tax on one of the following: (A) your actual profit, that is, total gross receipts less any expenses and capital allowances; or (B) your gross receipts over the Rent a Room limit, i.e. total gross receipts less £7,500. You can check out the UK Government and HMRC websites for the full details on the Rent a Room Scheme in all their glory.

Handling the legal aspects

Although taking in a lodger has fewer legal requirements than letting out a whole property, there are still some basic things you need to do to put the tenancy on a firm legal footing and manage the key risks involved. We'll spend a bit of time looking at these now, including what to do at the start of a tenancy and how to handle the eviction process, if things go wrong.

The start of the tenancy

As of 1 February 2016, the law requires everyone renting out property in England to check whether tenants are legally allowed to live in the UK – this is known as Right to Rent Checks. The law applies to landlords and to anyone letting out a room to a lodger. It requires you to check, within 28 days of the start of a tenancy, original copies of the documents that allow the tenant to live in the UK, make copies of these, and record the date you made the check. There is a Home Office guide to carrying out Right to Rent Checks on the gov.uk website.

Before you agree to let out your room or put a contract in place, you should consider carrying out the same background checks, e.g. on personal background, employment record, references and credit checks, that you would in a normal tenant-screening process. Websites like spareroom.co.uk and organisations like the National Residential Landlords Association (or NRLA) offer tenant referencing services that are well worth the money versus the time cost of doing this yourself.

The legal agreement

Although it's not technically required, I recommend putting any rental agreement in writing. This will protect both you and your lodger and give you a basis for reference, should any disagreements arise in the future. It's only when things go wrong that you'll be glad you did this.

Websites like spareroom.co.uk have template "Lodger Agreements" available for £7.50. These templates, drafted by solicitors, are suitable for most landlords in England & Wales and Scotland and can be a low-cost way of getting a basic agreement in place. Likewise, the NRLA provides templates on its website for their members. These template agreements include one for "excluded tenancies" – that is, for lodgers you share a living space such as a kitchen, living room, or bathroom with – which will be suitable for most purposes.

Ending a tenancy

Finally, you also need to think about what happens when the tenancy comes to an end. Although no-one likes to think about scenarios where things don't work out, it's helpful to know your legal rights to make sure you go about things the right way. Here's a summary of what you need to know.

If your lodger is an "excluded occupier" – meaning they live in your home and you or a family member share a kitchen, bathroom, or living room with them – you need to give them 'reasonable notice' to quit. Usually this means the length of the rental payment period, e.g. one week's notice if your tenant pays rent weekly. The notice itself does not have to be in writing.

If your lodger is an occupier with "basic protection" – meaning they live in your home and they do not share any living space with you – you must service them a written 'notice to quit'. The notice period will depend on the tenancy or agreement in place with your lodger, but is often at least four weeks. You can find out more about the legal aspects of taking in a lodger, handling deposits, and ending a tenancy, as well as information on things like how to handle a change of property ownership on the gov.uk website.

Pitfalls and common mistakes

The main pitfalls and mistakes landlords make with this strategy arise when they treat the whole process a bit too informally. Here are some common ones:

- Inadvertently creating a HMO – If you let out rooms to two or more people, you may have accidentally created a House in Multiple Occupation (HMO). There are extra safety requirements and standards for HMOs and you'll often need a license too. Make sure you don't fall foul of these regulations.
- Letting a room to a friend – Although letting out a room to a friend sounds like a great idea (who wouldn't want to live with their bestie), it isn't always a great idea in practice. For example, you might be inclined to cut your friend some slack if they can't pay the rent one month – something you're unlikely to do for a stranger. Remember, keep it professional.
- Violating the terms of your lease – Not all leasehold apartments will allow you to rent out part of your property in this manner. You need to check the terms of your lease to see if this strategy is viable. Letting out a room in a freehold house can be easier, as there are often less restrictions.

If forewarned is forearmed, as the saying goes, you should be able to avoid these mistakes yourself and reap the benefits this strategy has to offer. Over the long term, this play can have a meaningful impact on your personal finances and on your property journey. If it's done right, it can even allow you to live pretty much rent-free, maximising the amount of savings you can put towards new property investments. So, what are you waiting for? Don't let that spare room sit idle – put it to work and see what it can do for you.

Further reading and useful resources

If you're interested in this strategy, there are some great resources out there to help you put it into action. You might like to check out the following:

- The "Rent a room in your home" page on the gov.uk website
- The "Info & Advice for Landlords" page at spareroom.co.uk
- Additional information on the NRLA website at nrla.org.uk

HMRC also issue fresh guidance each year on the Rent a Room Scheme, so that you can make sure you're up-to-speed with all things tax-related.

Redux

You can extend this strategy to include a wide range of variants. In the modern gig economy, there's a whole host of websites and "peer-to-peer" rental platforms dedicated to letting out your spare stuff. Got a vehicle lying around idle? You can partner with hiyacar.co.uk or drivy.co.uk to rent out your car and generate some extra income. Got a spare parking space at your home? Try justpark.com. What about that digital SLR camera or that novelty drone you bought last Christmas? Look no further than fatllama.com. Pretty much whatever you have lying around, there's a website you can use to rent it out.

Play # 15 – Switch to an interest only mortgage

When she was growing up, Ruta's parents had always encouraged her to live within her means and avoid debt. When she bought her own home five years ago, she'd opted for a repayment mortgage – the idea of paying off the loan over time appeared prudent and sensible, even though an interest only loan was hundreds of pounds a month cheaper. One day, a friend challenged her logic, explaining that if she opted for an interest only mortgage and invested the cash savings, she'd be better off financially. Ruta began to wonder which of these viewpoints was correct.

How does it work?

There are only a few things you can do to lower you living expenses and free up extra resources to invest. We've already looked at baselining and budgeting – after we've exhausted those options, the interest only mortgage play is often the last tool we've got left. But it's one that can make a real difference to your monthly cash flow, if you get it right.

There are two main types of mortgage you can use to buy your own home – *repayment* and *interest only* mortgages. With a repayment mortgage, you pay off a small amount of the loan each month plus some interest. By the end of the term, you will have paid off the loan in full. With an interest only mortgage, you pay just the interest on the borrowed money each month. At the end of the mortgage term, you still owe the bank the original loan amount borrowed. So, you'll need a plan for how to pay this back at the end of the term. The monthly payments are higher for repayment mortgages than interest only mortgages, because you're paying off the loan gradually over time.

Most owner-occupiers take out repayment mortgages. Their thinking is that they want to have their mortgage paid off by the time they retire. So, they opt to pay it off gradually. This is the default for most residential property owners in the UK, and it's generally favoured by the banks. Property investors, however, often opt for interest only mortgages, where the monthly payments are lower, and their monthly cash flow position is better. So, which is the right option to use *with your own home,* and what does the investment case for making this switch look like? Let's take a deep dive on this issue.

The case for switching to interest only

If you find yourself with extra cash flow, you might be asking whether it's better to pay off your debts or invest those funds to generate a return. The answer to this question can be complex, and we've talked about this in play # 2. The same principle applies here though. That is, if the return you generate by investing the funds is higher than the interest accruing on the debt, then your net worth, i.e. your total assets less your total liabilities, will increase more quickly if you invest, rather than paying down debt.

How can we apply this principle to the decision on switching to an interest only mortgage? Well, if we go with a repayment mortgage, then we're choosing to pay off some of the mortgage balance each month. The relevant interest rate here is our mortgage interest rate, which could be around 2% p.a. in the current environment for a 75% loan-to-value mortgage. So, if I switch to an interest only mortgage, then I only need to achieve 2% p.a. or greater through my investment using that extra cash flow to be in a better position financially. With most buy-to-let property ventures, you'd definitely be hoping to achieve an ROI of 5% p.a. or more, and so it makes logical financial sense to make the switch to an interest only mortgage and use that extra cash flow to invest.

How much extra cash flow could it generate?

To understand how much extra cash flow this could free up for investment, it's useful to take a look at a worked example. Let's take another look at that two-bedroom apartment in Leeds City Centre from play # 13. In the table below, I've compared the monthly cost of buying the property with a repayment mortgage and an interest only mortgage.

Mortgage	Repayment	Interest only
Purchase price	£160,000	£160,000
Loan-to-value	75%	75%
Interest rate	2.0% p.a.	2.0% p.a.
Mortgage cost	£509	£200
Service charge	£125	£125
Ground rent	£30	£30
Maintenance	£50	£50
Total monthly cost	£714	£405

Here, the cost of owning the apartment is £714 with a repayment mortgage and £405 with an interest only mortgage. Switching to interest only therefore gives us a potential cash saving of £309 per month, which we can put back into future property investments.

Barriers to switching

Bank lending criteria

This play will not be available to everyone. Since the last financial crisis in 2007, banks have employed much stricter lending criteria, and the option of using an interest only mortgage to fund a residential home purchase is more restricted. HSBC, for example, currently require applicants to be earning £100,000 or more per annum, excluding bonus, commission, overtime and rental income. Barclays are applying a lower income threshold of £75,000 for interest only mortgage applicants; Halifax currently have no income threshold, but do require applicants to prove they have a plan in place for paying off the outstanding loan balance at the end of the mortgage term. So, not everyone will have this option open to them. In the current environment, it's best to speak to a mortgage broker to see what options are available given your circumstances.

The banks will also apply other lending criteria based on the type of property you're looking to purchase. The main constraint here is likely to be the maximum loan-to-value the banks will permit for an interest only mortgage. At the time of writing, this is typically 75% for most lenders, meaning you'll need a deposit of 25% or more to go down this route. It also means if you're currently on a repayment mortgage, you'll need to have accrued equity of at least 25% in the property to make the switch, otherwise you might have to put in further funds to make up the difference. In the latter case, it's unlikely to make financial sense to inject additional funds, given the point of making the switch in the first place is the free up some additional funds to invest. If you're in this position, you're probably better sticking with your existing repayment mortgage.

The mental barrier

If you're not overly comfortable with the general idea of debt, then a repayment mortgage might appear to be a safer choice. Many people like the idea of paying down the loan balance each month, even if they know that it makes more financial sense to go down the interest only route and reinvest the extra cash flow. The allure of being debt-free by retirement is strong, and for many people it's strong enough to prevent them from making the switch.

Although it's really a matter of personal preference, I'd like to provide some counterbalance to this tendency to stick with the repayment mortgage. The first leg of my argument is a practical one – if your plan is to grow a large property portfolio, then you'll be able to do this much faster if you opt for an interest only mortgage and reinvest that extra cash. The second leg is one around flexibility – a repayment mortgage *commits* you to having to pay off some of the loan balance each month. With an interest only mortgage, I can still *choose* to use the extra cash flow to pay down the balance, but I don't have to. So, because of this extra flexibility, the interest only option is safer from a cash flow perspective. The third and final leg of this tripod is about leverage. We know leverage can dramatically enhance our returns in an environment where property prices are rising. Yet with a repayment mortgage, we're reducing our leverage by paying down some of the mortgage balance each month. So, if you believe property prices will continue to rise over the long term, you'll maximise your overall returns if you go with an interest only mortgage, thereby maximising your leverage.

Getting over this mental barrier to switching is as important as meeting the banks' lending criteria in the first place. If you're not convinced after reading the above, then I don't know if there's anything else I can say to persuade you. At the end of the day, this is an idea you'll need to get comfortable with yourself before you make the switch. And to the brave souls who do make the leap, all credit to you for breaking the mould and daring to do things differently.

Play # 16 – Flip your own home for a profit

Carla's path to building wealth via property was a little different than most people. She wasn't a great saver and she hadn't invested in buy-to-lets. She was, however, a dab hand at DIY and she had an eye for design, which she'd put to good use in home renovation projects. Over six years, she moved house three times, each time buying properties in need of serious TLC, refurbishing them to a high standard, and selling them on for a profit. Also, because it was her own home, she paid no capital gains tax. She'd taken on these projects for love, not money, but they enabled her to build serious wealth nonetheless. She had fun doing what she loved and got paid handsomely to do it. What's not to like?

Why flip your own home

If flipping properties for a profit is the kind of thing that gets your juices flowing, then you should definitely consider play # 16. Flipping your own home for profit offers a range of advantages to the would-be developer, and it can be a great first step in your journey, provided you do this in the right way. As with play # 13, the trick here is to make sure the property you choose works as a home (at least on a temporary basis) and stacks up as a profitable refurbishment project.

Flipping your home is a great way to get started in property development. It helps you build up your experience and your track record in a relatively low risk setting, i.e. without the pressure of expensive bridging financing (more on this later) bearing down on every overrun and delay. What's more, there's something about the idea of flipping your own home that, for many new investors, feels more achievable than flipping a property that's further from where you live and is that little bit more remote.

To execute this strategy successfully, you'll need to take into account the same factors as a regular property flip and approach the project in the same way. We'll cover all that detail in play # 25, so I won't repeat it again here. In this section, we'll simply concentrate on those aspects of property flipping that are unique to flipping your own home. Let's start off with some of the key advantages you'll get if you choose to use your home in this way.

Advantages to flipping your own home

It can be a tax efficient

The general idea of property flips is to buy a property, refurbish it and sell it on for more than you spent on it. As such, anything that lowers your purchase costs or increases your sale proceeds will add to the profit you make.

If you don't own any other properties at this point, then you won't be subject to the 3% stamp duty surcharge paid on second properties in the UK, which will lower your purchase costs. In addition, you don't pay capital gains tax when you sell your main UK residence, meaning you'll get to keep all of the profit you make. Taken together, flipping your own home can, therefore, be tax efficient.

Potential cost savings

On a home refurbishment project, you'll be living in the property and you'll be around when the works are going on. This presents a range of opportunities for potential cost savings. Depending on your skillset, you might be able to take care of project management and coordinating the input from various tradespeople. You might also be able to do some of the works yourself, e.g. painting, decorating, or more complex tasks, if you have the ability and the confidence to taken this on.

At the bare minimum, you should be able to help with basic tasks like clearing-out any junk and tidying up afterwards, all of which can lower your costs.

Lower money down

You're purchasing your own home, so the capital requirements tend to be lower. You might be able to get away with a 10% deposit, rather than needing to put down 25% or more of the purchase price, i.e. what you'd require with traditional bridging finance. Flipping this around then, for a fixed sum of capital, a lower 10% deposit would mean you could purchase a higher value property in the first place, increasing the price range for potential flip projects.

It's also worth noting that when you're flipping your own home, there may be other sources of finance open to you that would not otherwise be there. You might be able to make use of personal loans to finance some of the development costs or even to put some of the bills on your credit card. These extra options can help lower your overall capital requirements.

Extends your range of projects

When you flip your own home, you'll pay mortgage costs, which are cheaper than the cost of bridging finance used in traditional flips. In addition, you'll be living in the property, so you'll be saving on rent. Both of these factors will keep your base run rate costs for the development low, so you can afford to take on projects with a slightly longer time horizon than with regular flips and keep them profitable. This would include, for example, projects where planning permission is expected to be a lengthy process or where there is uncertainty around whether it will be granted at all.

Peace of mind

Finally, there's the peace of mind that flipping your own home can bring. Because you're around to oversee the works, this can bring an extra layer of comfort to the project that you wouldn't get with a normal flip. You'll be there to scrutinise every little detail and to see the progress that's being made on a daily basis. This level of oversight and attention gives you the best possible chance of making the project a success and getting the outcome you desire.

Common pitfalls and mistakes

The main pitfalls and mistakes that arise with this are when people forget to treat the purchase as a business venture. Here are some common ones:

- Paying too much – If you pay too much for the property, this will negatively impact your profits. This is easier to do when buying a home you'll live in yourself, as the decision can be more emotional.
- Not developing an exit strategy – As with a regular property flip, you need to make sure there's a strong pool of potential buyers there when you come to sell. Make sure you have a robust exit strategy in place.
- Furnishing and redecoration – You need to do this in a way that's suitable for the end market. Don't buy overly expensive or lavish furniture unless you're confident this is what buyers want and they're prepared to pay for it.

There are also a couple of things you'll need to watch out for on the financing side. Technically, mortgage financing is not to be used for refurbishments – that's the purpose of bridging finance. So, if you plan to use a mortgage, be careful. Whilst you might get away with one flip every few years, it will start to look suspicious if you're flipping a property every six months, in which case I'd suggest you look into using bridging finance instead. Also, make sure you understand any early repayment charges and factor in these costs as well.

Reversal

This strategy is best suited for someone with strong project management skills and a background in property development. It can also be a great help if you have connections with tradespeople – e.g. builders, electricians, plumbers, decorators

– and if you have a background in interior design or some other relevant field. It goes without saying that if you don't have these skills, think carefully about taking on a project like this. Don't take on a project you can't handle; remember to start out simple and build up your experience gradually.

This strategy also requires a strong level of determination and commitment. You'll likely be living in or around a building site for a considerable length of time, which is not to everyone's taste. In addition, some people will simply be in a life position where this kind of strategy is impossible. For example, you might have elderly relatives that live with you, some kind of pet that might tear up the place, or you might live and work in an area that's unsuitable for this type of project. You should keep this under review over time, as circumstances change, meaning even if this play doesn't work for you right now, it may well do so in the future.

Play # 17 – Discover alternative sources of finance

When Bryn moved to Leeds to take a graduate job after university, he was keen to get on the property ladder right away. He'd stashed around £5,000 of his student loan over the course of his degree, and he also decided to take the £7,000 interest free loan his new employer was offering and put it to good use. All in, he had around £12,000 to play with as a deposit. Within six months of starting his new job, Bryn managed to secure a lovely little one-bedroom apartment overlooking the Leeds Liverpool Canal within walking distance of the city centre. Not a bad result six months into his working life and a result he'd achieved without too much personal sacrifice. It was a great start to his working life and his property journey.

Fast track your progress

There's lots of talk in the property industry about various shortcuts to success, including things like no-money-down deals. In general, I don't believe these kinds of shortcuts are possible, and I've always tended to steer clear of anyone spouting overtly optimistic rhetoric about the ability to do deals without needing any resources at all. In my experience, this is just not true. However, there is a place in every property investor's toolkit for creative uses of everyday financing options, and we're going to take a look at some of those options here.

Alternative sources of finance

By alternative sources, we're talking about any options other than traditional mortgages and bridging finance. You can use alternatives like these to reduce the amount of cash required to invest in a buy-to-let property deal or finance a flip and to help speed up your progress. So, without further ado, let's take a look at some of the options available and how you might use them.

Bank of mum and dad

If you're looking for some extra funds to finance your next property deal, look no further than the bank of mum and dad. In all seriousness, if your parents are in a position to help you out and if they're happy to do so, this can be a great way to accelerate your property journey and get things moving sooner.

It's usually easier to persuade mum and dad to lend if you're buying your own home rather than doing a buy-to-let or a flip, but there's no reason they can't help you out with those too. I would always advocate paying them back, i.e. treating it as a loan rather than a gift and setting out in writing how much you're borrowing and when you plan to pay them back i.e. agreeing a repayment plan. You should think about whether the loan is interest free or not. If you do decide to pay them interest, then there may be tax implications.

If your parents are keen on gifting monies to you, then make sure to check out the rules around inheritance tax and gifts, including the rules on exempted gifts, the annual exemption, and taper relief. If your parents own assets in excess of the inheritance tax threshold, they may be keen to gift assets to you earlier, as it can lead to inheritance tax savings. A financial planner will be able to help here.

Finally, please do make sure you treat any requests for funds with the utmost seriousness and respect. You should be clear what you're asking your parents to provide, and, if it's an investment project, take them through your business plan. Your parents have every right to say no, even if they do have the funds available. Be patient, give them time to think about what you're offering, and above all show your appreciation – say thank you.

Personal Loans

Personal loans are another great source of funds outside of traditional mortgages. A personal loan is an arrangement to borrow money over a fixed term. You pay the loan back via monthly instalments at a fixed interest rate. They're generally unsecured, meaning you're not asked to provide collateral and they're repayable over a period of up to seven years.

You need to be careful how you use the loan, as most lenders will not allow the funds to be used to purchase property or land, which rules out using this as a deposit. What's more, lenders don't usually permit you to take out a personal loan to cover everyday living expenses, which rules out using a personal loan to cover your bills and then save your wages instead.

So, what can they be used for? Well, personal loans can be used for things like home improvements such as a new bathroom or kitchen. This means you could potentially use one to finance a home refurbishment. In addition, you'll often be able use them for things like buying a car, paying for one-off events like weddings, or perhaps to pay for a once-in-a-lifetime holiday. As such, there may be ways to juggle your outgoings and expenditure to make use of personal loans in a way that facilitates your next property deal. I'll say no more than that.

Graduate and student loans

If you're a younger property investor, then graduate loans and student loans are another potential source of finance. Let's take a look at how these work.

Graduate loans are a type of loan offered by employers to university students starting out on a new graduate programme. These loans, which can be up to say £7,000, are interest free and are typically repayable over four years from your salary. There are no conditions around how you use the funds, so you're free to use it however you like. Just remember that because they need to be repaid over four years or so, they will lower your take-home pay, so you're effectively gaining advanced access to future savings.

If you're anything like me when I was a student, you'll have spent your student loan on CDs, movies, and nights out. However, if you have a little more foresight than me, you might decide you want to put that student loan to more productive uses. It'll be difficult to start investing while you're a student, after all you'll likely have no demonstrable income, so it will be difficult to get a mortgage. But there's no reason you can't save a student loan for later, pool it with another investor's funds, or look for other ways to secure the rest of the financing you'll need, e.g. a parental guarantee. If you put your mind to it, you can accomplish anything.

Credit cards and bank overdrafts

If you have a good job and a decent salary, then you might be able to secure some decent lines of credit with your bank via credit cards and bank overdrafts.

When you first take out a credit card, your credit limit will likely be capped at a few thousand pounds, but it's possible to extend this over time, provided your repayment history is good. Over a number of years, you might find it's possible to extend your credit limit to £10,000 or more and to secure an overdraft of £2,500 or higher. In total, that's a line of credit worth £12,500 or more that you could put to good use if you ever need to. Combine it with your partner's and you could be looking at £25,000 plus of finance right at your fingertips.

Credit cards and overdrafts are an expensive source of finance, with annual interest rates on the borrowing typically well above 10%. In general, you won't want to borrow on a credit card or dip into your overdraft for very long, so you should plan how and when to use this type of finance. If you're at the end of a refurb project that's expected to complete in a few weeks and you need to buy a new kitchen, you could consider paying for it on a credit card, with the plan to pay off the credit card balance when the property sells. Equally, you might be able to use a credit card to pay for certain fees incurred in the buying process, e.g. fees charged by auctioneers or solicitors, or at least use it to cover some of your living expenses and free up some cash on a temporary basis.

If you do find that you're running a higher credit card balance for longer than expected, you could consider using a balance transfer credit card. These cards often charge no interest on your balance for up to 24 months after the transfer. Watch out for the transfer fees though, which can be around 3% of the balance. Also, take care to minimise the impact of this sort of borrowing on your overall credit rating.

Reversal

I'm all for creative uses of personal finance options, but you need to make sure you're playing within the bounds of what's fair and legitimate. If you find yourself pushing things too far, i.e. the only way to get a deal done is to borrow some from your parents, take out a personal loan, and stick the rest on a credit card, you're probably pushing it too far. If that sounds like you, maybe take a step back, think about how to increase your savings, and try to be a little more patient. It's okay to wait a little longer to do that next deal.

The biggest mistake I see people making is pushing their personal and family relationships too far. It's one thing to take on a risky project if the risk is all your own, but it's another if you're risking money that your family and friends have lent to you in good faith. In all your dealings with friends and family, treat them professionally and like you would any business partner. If they aren't onboard with your plans or see them as too risky, don't force them to help you out You might be risking more than your next property deal.

Play # 18 – The young professional landlord

The Northern Quarter, Manchester's creative, urban heartland, is home to trendy fashion stores, record shops, bars and restaurants. When Dave moved to the city to take a job as an insurance broker, he wanted to be right in the middle of it, but he also wanted to ride the Manchester property wave, which in recent years had gathered serious momentum. When a couple of friends suggested living together, he wondered if there was a way to do both.

How does it work?

This play is the first of our combination plays. It brings together play # 14, earn extra cash letting out a spare room, and play # 17, discover alternative sources of finance, in a play I call the young professional landlord. The general idea is to buy a house or flat as your own home that would work well as shared accommodation for young professionals, e.g. a three-bedroom house or apartment near to a city. Then you take one of the bedrooms, and you rent out the other two.

There's a time in life for most young people, that period straight after college or university when you've just started work in your first job and where renting is the de facto accommodation choice. This play is our answer to the generation rent conundrum, and it can help the aspiring property investor to start accruing wealth through property sooner than might otherwise be possible. This play has two principal aims and objectives.

1. To help you to save more – If you get this play right, you might be able to cut down your accommodation costs to nil, allowing you to save more.
2. To help you build up some equity – Any equity you accrue in your own home can be re-used later to fund additional property investments.

The beauty of this play is that it's actually not restricted to young professionals. As long as you're prepared to share your home with a couple of strangers, there's no reason you couldn't put it into action at any stage in your life, though it might be more difficult to do this if you already have a family and children.

A worked example

Suppose you were a young professional about to take a job in Leeds city centre. Rather than renting a one-bedroom apartment in the city centre, arguably money down the drain, you could consider buying a three-bedroom house in Headingley. This is an area outside the city – it's a 15 to 20-minute bus ride from the city centre and a 10 to 15-minute walk from Leeds University and Leeds General Infirmary – with plenty of potential tenants looking for rooms to rent.

Here's an illustration of the kinds of figures involved, based on a real-life example from a work colleague who carried out this play. The key assumptions here are as follows: (a) that we can secure a three-bedroom house in Headingley for £200,000, which is a little aggressive, but not unachievable; (b) we purchase the property with a 90% loan-to-value repayment mortgage with an interest rate of 2% p.a. repayable over a 30 year term; (c) that we will cover all the cost of the household bills and add an allowance for bills onto the price we charge our tenants; (d) that we can let out two of the rooms for £350 rent plus £100 for bills, i.e. £450 per calendar month; (e) that we'll do all the marketing of the rooms and viewings ourselves, but we'll pay a company to carry out tenant reference checks, and we'll pay for some legal templates to get a decent lodger agreement in place with each of the tenants. The numbers then work out as follows:

Monthly income

Rental income plus bills (bedroom 1)	£450
Rental income plus bills (bedroom 2)	£450
Total income	£900

Monthly expenditure

Mortgage cost	£665
Council tax	£100
Water bills	£60
Heating and electricity	£100
Broadband and Netflix subscription	£40
Buildings and public liability insurance	£30
Voids (£900 per month × 2 / 52 weeks)	£35
Tenant reference checks	£10
Total expenditure	£1,040

I've ignored the cost of repairs here, as these are costs you'd have to deal with anyway as a homeowner, and I'm assuming we've picked a property in good repair. I've also assumed each of the rooms is vacant for an average of two weeks per year, which is akin to a tenant staying for two years and then the room taking a month or so to let out again.

In this example, we generate £900 per month of income to cover our monthly expenditure of £1,040. That is, we've cut our accommodation costs to £140 per month, which helps us meet our first objective of saving more each month. In addition, because we've taken out a repayment mortgage, we're building equity in the property. If you enter the figures above into your favourite online mortgage calculator, you'll see that after five years, we'll have paid off around £23,000 of the original loan amount, meaning at a time in life when most people are renting, we will build up £23,000 of equity in our home that we can recycle and re-use later to expand our portfolio. That's a tick in the box for objective number two of building some equity.

You can potentially push the figures above even further. In this illustration, we've assumed a 30-year repayment term, but if the bank allowed you to extend this out to 35 years or more, you could potentially cut your mortgage payments by £70 per month, bringing your accommodation costs virtually to nil. The term of the mortgage is a variable you can play around with yourself when you come to execute this strategy in practice.

Other considerations

A word or two on tax

As in play # 14, earn extra cash letting out a spare room, the Rent a Room Scheme will let you earn £7,500 per year tax-free letting out furnished accommodation in your own home. In the example above, we're expecting to earn over £7,500 in a year, so you might end up paying a little tax.

Also, it's worth being aware that there are some potential capital gains tax implications. When you come to sell your home, the gain on the part of your home that's used for letting is liable to capital gains tax, because you'll have had two lodgers. How much of the gain is taxed is usually based on the percentage floor area let out and the amount of time the property was let for as a proportion of the total time you owned the property. There would be no need for such a calculation if you had only one lodger at a time, as having a single lodger does not count as letting your home for business purposes, whereas have two or more lodgers does. Make sure to check this out with your accountant.

Financing the deal

The worked example above assumes you have a £20,000 deposit available to do this deal. In practice, you should make use of all the financing options available to you, including those that we covered in our previous play, like the bank of mum and dad, graduate or student loans, and any savings you've managed to build up in prior years.

If a three-bedroom house is a stretch at this point, you could consider opting for a two-bedroom, one-lodger version of the example above, which might still offer some of the same benefits, i.e. reduce your accommodation costs and build up some equity, albeit on a smaller scale. If this is the limit of what your finances will allow at this point in your life, then it's better than nothing, and it will be a darned site better for your finances than doing nothing. Get creative and try to come up with the best proposition you can.

Keys to success

Many of the same keys to success, common pitfalls and mistakes will apply here as for play # 14 and play # 17, so I won't repeat those again here. Here are some of the other keys to success that apply here.

- Pick tenants carefully – Even more so than when you take in a lodger, picking the right tenants is crucial. Your tenants should, ideally, be at a similar stage in life to you and looking for a similar lifestyle. Again, it's usually best to steer clear of friends or colleagues, even though it might sound like fun.

- Stay on top of repairs – You should attend to any repairs promptly and stay on top of any maintenance issues. That way, your tenants will be more likely to stay longer, and you'll maximise your income. In short, treat this like any other business, and you won't go far wrong.

- Write some house rules – You're living with more than one person, so you might want to write some house rules. These could cover use of communal areas like kitchens and bathrooms, any shared costs, e.g. milk, bread, and any rules around guests staying over, playing music, and lights out.

- Bills and shared costs – In practice, it's usually easier to charge for costs like council tax, utility bills, telephone and broadband as a lump sum added to the monthly rent, rather than trying to allocate them out. Just be clear on what shared costs are covered in the rental agreement.

Also, remember that to make use of the Rent a Room Scheme, the rooms need to be furnished. So, you'll need to make sure each room is appropriately furnished and that you're covering the cost of any replacement furniture needed.

Redux

You can extend this strategy to include a range of variants. If you're moving to university and you have the backing of mum and dad, e.g. if they gift you a deposit, act as a guarantor for your mortgage, or allow you to take a second mortgage charge on their home (play # 23) then you could arguably do the same thing as a student. Equally, if you're a bit older, divorced and trying to make a new start in life, this strategy could work for you too, with a slightly older clientele.

Play # 19 – The home extension strategy

The garden at the back of Ellie's home in Banbury was a generous size and it wasn't overlooked by the neighbours. Other people in the neighbourhood had already extended their homes, and she figured there was a good chance she'd be able to get planning permission for a self-contained flat at the back of the property. Over a number of years, the income from renting out the flat would pay for the cost of the build itself, and it would also make a great little granny flat for her mum in a few years' time.

How does it work?

This play is our second combination play. It brings together play # 14, earn extra cash letting out a spare room, and play # 17, discover alternative sources of finance, in a play I call the home extension strategy. The idea is to take a home you already own that has room for an extension, extend it to create one or more extra bedrooms, then rent out the additional rooms.

Though it's based on a similar idea to the last play, this strategy accomplishes the same thing in a different manner. It's less about buying a suitable property and living in a shared house with other young professionals, and it's more about using your property development skills and a bit of imagination to create the equivalent of an extra rental property within your own home. Unlike the previous play, this one is actually quite well-suited to families and couples who are more likely to own a suitable house that's capable of being extended in the right way to make this work. This play has three principal aims:

1. Positive cash flow – If you get the numbers right, this play should generate some positive cash flow for you each month and improve your finances.
2. To help build some equity – Your new lodgers will help you pay off the loan needed to finance the build and help you grow equity that can be re-used.
3. Get some development experience – It's a great way to help build up some property development experience and improve your skills in this area.

The beauty of this play is that it achieves two of the key aims of most property investment strategies, i.e. positive cash flow and extra equity, and it can be done with relatively modest cash requirements from the investor. Let's take a look at a worked example.

A worked example

Suppose you're a young family living in a commuter town outside of Bristol. The area is a 20-minute bus ride into Bristol city centre and it's in an area with plenty of tenant demand. You own a three-bedroom house that has a flat-roof, double garage, and it's a good enough size that you could potentially extend over the garage and create a couple of extra ensuite double bedrooms.

This example is based on one from a good friend of mine who's also a fellow property investor. The key background to the example is as follows: (a) that the double garage is 6m by 6m and we'll turn this into two 3m by 6m double rooms with an ensuite shower for each room; (b) that the cost of the extension is £40,000 (around £1,000 per sq-m for a single storey) including costs associated with design and planning approvals; (c) we fund the cost of the extension using £10,000 of our savings and a loan of £30,000 at an interest rate of 3.5% p.a. that we'll pay back over seven years; (d) that we will cover the cost of the household bills and add an allowance for bills onto the price we charge our tenants for the rooms; (e) that we can let out the two rooms for £400 rent plus £100 for bills, i.e. £500 per calendar month. The numbers then work out as follows:

Monthly income

Rental income plus bills (bedroom 1)	£500
Rental income plus bills (bedroom 2)	£500
Total income	£1,000

Monthly expenditure

Loan repayment	£403
Council tax	£100
Water bills	£60
Heating and electricity	£100
Broadband and Netflix subscription	£40
Buildings and public liability insurance	£30
Voids (£1,000 per month × 2 / 52 weeks)	£38
Tenant reference checks	£10
Total expenditure	£781

I've ignored the cost of repairs here, as these are costs you'd have to deal with anyway as a homeowner. I've also assumed each of the rooms is vacant for an average of two weeks per year, which is akin to a tenant staying for two years and then the room taking a month or so to let out again. You may be able to do better than this, if you're proactive on the marketing.

In this example, we would generate £1,000 of income per month versus our monthly expenditure of £781. That is, we would generate £219 cash flow each month or around £2,628 of annual profit before tax. To see what this equates to as an ROI, we simply take the annual profit of £2,628 ÷ £10,000 (the money we put into the development ourselves) which equals 26.3% before tax. That's not a bad ROI in the current world where interest rates are close to zero, and it's also a tick in the box for the first of our three key objectives.

Now let's fast forward seven years after we've paid back the original loan of £30,000. At this point, our monthly loan repayment of £403 will disappear and our pre-tax profit will increase to £622 per month or £7,464 per year. That's a strong ROI of £7,464 ÷ £10,000 equals 74.6%. What's more, at this point we've paid off the loan, so we've accrued £30,000 of additional equity in our own home that we can re-use later to expand our property portfolio. That's a tick in the box for objective number two as well.

You can potentially push the figures above even further. You might be able to borrow the entire amount needed to finance the build, rather than needing to put in any cash savings yourself. In this case, your pre-tax ROI would effectively be infinite, and you would have gained £40,000 of additional equity in your own home that's paid for by your new lodgers. You can play around with different combinations of money down, amount borrowed, and the term of the loan to produce a set of figures you're happy with.

Other considerations

Tax considerations

As for play # 14, earn extra cash letting out a spare room, the Rent a Room Scheme will let you earn £7,500 per year tax-free letting out furnished accommodation in your own home. In the example above, we're expecting to earn over £7,500 in the year, so you might end up paying some tax here. This will lower your post-tax ROI and you should consider this in your calculations too.

It's worthwhile thinking about the tax position for other development types. For example, the Rent a Room Scheme only applies if you're a resident landlord, and you can't use the scheme for homes converted into separate, self-contained flats. As such, if your home extension strategy is to develop separate flats on the side, it will likely be taxed as a regular buy-to-let investment. However, if you have a family and you'd prefer to keep your tenants' living space separate from your own, then this may be your preferred option.

Financing the development costs

There are various options available to finance the development, but the two most commonly used options are personal loans and homeowner loans. We've already covered personal loans in play # 17, so we won't cover that again here. But it's worth pointing out that the example calculation above was based on a seven-year personal loan at an interest rate of 3.5%, which is pretty typical of personal loan products available in the market at the time of writing.

A homeowner loan is a secured loan that enables you to use any equity you have built up in your own home as security for a fresh loan. Let's look at a simple example. Say your home was valued at £200,000 and you had a mortgage balance of £120,000 outstanding, then you have accrued £80,000 worth of equity. You can pledge this equity as security for the homeowner loan.

This type of homeowner loan is usually available from separate lenders other than your current mortgage provider. The rates are often more competitive than for unsecured personal loans and they can often be repaid over ten years or more, meaning they may be the preferred option for any projects which have higher development costs and where you want to spread out the repayment over a much longer period.

Finally, if you've accrued some equity in your own home over time, you could also consider re-mortgaging as a way to unlock the funds needed to carry out the extension works. We cover re-mortgaging in more detail in Volume 2.

Keys to success

There are a number of prerequisites to executing this strategy. Firstly, you need to own a house, a piece of land, or some other kind of property where this type of home extension strategy is possible. Secondly, you need to live in an area where the rental income achievable is high relative to the cost of the extension itself. At the time of writing, that's likely to be more true in the South of England than it is in the North of England, as rents tend to be higher in the south and the cost of carrying out the extension works is largely insensitive to the location. Here are some of the other keys to success for this particular play.

- Strong project management – If you have strong project management skills and prior development experience, that will make the whole process much easier. You'll be able to track progress, keep the pressure on when things go off-track, and adjust decisions in real-time to keep your costs in check.
- Stay resilient – Anyone who's lived through a home extension will tell you that it can be pretty disruptive to everyday life. You need to stay mentally resilient and try to remember that your house won't always look like a building site – the project will end eventually.
- Have extra funds available – If you've ever watched Grand Designs with Kevin McCloud, there's usually a hairy moment when the build is about to run out of funds, possibly for dramatic effect and enhanced TV viewing. Make sure this doesn't happen to you and that you have cash to cover overruns.

As for play # 16, flip your own home for a profit, this strategy is best suited for someone with strong project management skills and existing connections with the building trade. However, if you're keen enough and if it's a project you fancy taking on, it's a great place to start building up your development experience. That's a tick in the box for the last of our three objectives and one of the best pre-tax ROIs you might see in the whole of property.

Part Three : Making your first investments

Play # 20 – The basic buy-to-let investment

Hugh's job as a corporate M&A lawyer in the city was demanding and time intensive. He would often have to drop whatever he was doing at a moment's notice to deal with some emergency or another back at the office. The one saving grace was that it allowed him to save lots, something he was keen to take advantage of through his property investments. Being time poor, Hugh's strategy was focussed around acquiring buy-to-let investments that were ready-to-go and where he could outsource the day-to-day management to a letting agent. The last thing he needed was another time drag.

As simple as porridge

The vanilla buy-to-let investment is the workhorse of many a property portfolio. It's the jumping-off point for many new investors, and it's the play experienced investors often come back to later in their career, after making money in other property ventures. If you save hard, start investing young, and use the power of compounding to your advantage, you can accomplish great things and achieve financial freedom with nothing more than this one play.

In this section, we're going to take a look at the simplest possible version of buy-to-let – that is, we're going to look at buying a ready-made investment that needs little-to-no-work, the key decisions you'll need to make along the way, and what results are possible if you take this approach. This strategy is well-suited to investors with a high monthly savings rate, but who are time-poor. What's more, being a mini business in its own right, the basic buy-to-let is also a great starting point for learning about property investment more generally.

To succeed with this play, you'll need to buy well, manage the property with care and attention over time, and sweat your new asset hard to make sure you're achieving the best possible investment returns. If this is your first real property investment, things are about to get exciting.

How to assess a deal

The idea behind the basic buy-to-let investment is simple – you buy a property and you let it out to a tenant, typically for a period of six months or more, in return for the tenant paying rent. The principal motivation for investing is to generate a monthly income or cash flow, but many investors using this strategy also hope to achieve some capital growth over the long term.

Return on investment ("ROI")

Return on investment or ROI is our best guess at the return we're going to achieve on the property. It shows us how hard our money is working for us, and it's what we're going to use to decide whether a particular deal is a good one.

ROI is calculated as the annual rental profit from the property divided by the cash invested in the deal. So, in order to calculate it, we'll need good estimates of the rental income from the property, the expenses associated with running it, and the amount of cash we have invested in the deal. Let's take a look at a worked example, based on a potential deal I was assessing recently in Leeds.

The property was a two-bedroom, two-bathroom apartment located 10 to 15 minutes' walk from Leeds City Centre. It was on the market for £170,000, but I felt I could potentially secure the deal for £160,000 with a strong negotiation strategy. The other key assumptions are as follows: (a) that the property would rent out for £825 per month, based on a quick search on Rightmove; (b) the estate agent provided me with the annual service charge of £1,200 and the annual ground rent of £240; (c) I would use a local letting agent to manage the property who would charge 12% of the rent; (d) repairs will cost 2.5% of the monthly rent; (e) costs for marketing and finding new tenants will be around £360 per annum; (f) to finance the deal I would use a 75% loan-to-value interest only mortgage at a 3% p.a. interest rate; (g) I would furnish the property before letting it out at a cost of around £2,000. Converting all these figures to monthly and adding in a few other costs that might be expected for a rental property like this, the numbers then work out as follows:

Rental income	£825

Monthly expenditure

Mortgage interest (3% × £120,000 ÷ 12)	£300
Service charge (£1,200 ÷ 12)	£100
Ground rent (£240 ÷ 12)	£20
Management fee (12% × £825)	£99
Repairs and maintenance (2.5% × £825)	£21
Cost of voids (£825 × 2 / 52 weeks)	£32
Public liability insurance (£60 p.a. ÷ 12)	£5
Marketing and tenancy set-up (£360 p.a. ÷ 12)	£30
Other costs (e.g. gas safety check)	£10
Total expenditure	£617

Cash invested

Deposit (25% × £160,000)	£40,000
Stamp duty	£5,500
Furnishing costs	£2,000
Valuation and survey	£500
Legal expenses	£1,500
Mortgage broker	£500
Total cash invested	£50,000

I've assumed that the property is vacant for an average of two weeks per year, which is akin to a tenant staying for two years on average and then the flat taking a month or so to let out again. In the cash invested section, I've also included typical allowances for stamp duty, legal expenses, valuation and broker fees.

In this example, we would achieve £825 of rental income versus our monthly expenses of £617. That is, we would generate £208 of cash flow each month or around £2,496 of annual profit before tax. To see what this equates to as an ROI, we simply take the annual profit of £2,496 ÷ £50,000 (i.e. the money we put into the deal ourselves) which equals 5.0% p.a. before tax.

When you work through a calculation of the ROI on a live deal, you should do everything you can to get the figures as accurate as possible. Speak to local agents about the potential rental income and do your own research on what similar properties have let out for on Rightmove. For flats and apartments, make sure you've got good estimates of the service charges and ground rent, based on past charges. Above all, make sure your estimates of the potential monthly profit are conservative – that is, err on the low side for the estimated rental income and on the high side for the expenses. That way, you won't be disappointed.

Factoring in capital growth

So far in this play, we've just looked at how to estimate the potential rental profit from the investment. However, for many property investors, capital growth is the reason they invest in property, not just the monthly returns. So how can we factor this into our decision making?

In practice, many investors are prepared to accept a lower ROI if they expect a particular property will achieve strong capital growth in the future. To illustrate this point, the table below shows the ROI a property investor might be prepared to accept on a basic, residential buy-to-let investment in the UK right now. That is, it shows how an investor might flex their investment criteria depending on their view about the capital growth potential for a particular property.

Growth potential	High	Medium	Low
ROI	5% - 8% p.a.	7% - 10% p.a.	9% - 12% p.a.

For example, say you feel confident that the property price and market rent for the above property in Leeds will continue to grow strongly for years to come. Then you may choose to accept an ROI of 5% p.a. today, even though there are lots of higher yielding investment properties out there. You wouldn't be alone in this decision, and there are many investors who would do the same.

In short, you can and you should flex the investment criteria that you apply, i.e. the ROI you're prepared to accept, depending on your views around the future growth prospects for a property and for a particular area.

Using ROI to set your price

You can also use ROI to set the maximum price that you're prepared to pay for a property. Let's take a look at how this works.

Suppose you've decided that a particular property needs to achieve an ROI of 6% p.a. to get us interested in doing a deal. You can play around with the purchase price in your calculation spreadsheet (if you don't have one of these, see the free resources section at the end of the book) until the ROI equals 6% p.a. This is then the maximum price you're prepared to pay for the property.

There's no guarantee that the seller will be interested in selling to you at the price you want to pay, of course. However, this technique can help us to set our walk-away point before we enter into negotiations. This can be extremely helpful in managing your emotions and making sure you don't overpay for the property in the heat of the moment.

Some important decisions

Although it's a simple and straightforward strategy, there are still a number of important decisions you need to make about how you will execute this play. Let's take a look at a number of the key ones.

- Income versus capital growth – Your strategy needs to align with your overall property goals. If your goals are all about income and cash flow generation, you'll want to focus on maximising the ROI you achieve. If your goals are all about wealth creation, you may choose to focus on capital growth.

- Whether to invest locally or not – It's unlikely your local area is the best place to invest at every point in time, so investing further afield is likely to give you the best chance of achieving strong returns. However, there might be reasons to stay local, e.g. strong local knowledge and a strong local network.

- To self-manage or use a letting agent – If you're time poor or investing away from your local area, appointing a letting agent to manage the property for you is likely the best option. Managing your properties yourself, however, can add hundreds of pounds a month to your cash flow.

- Furnished or unfurnished – Whether to furnish your properties is a decision that should be based on what the local market wants. In general, apartments in city centres will need to be furnished; family homes in the suburbs are best left unfurnished. Speak to a local letting agent to get their views.

- Tenant type – You should have in mind an ideal tenant type when you choose a property to buy. Letting out a property to young professionals, families, or tenants on benefits are all very different prospects. You need to think about what type of property portfolio you want to build.

These are just some of the decisions you'll need to make along the way as you develop your buy-to-let strategy. Other decisions are around whether to buy flats versus houses, how much leverage to use in financing your portfolio, and whether to accept tenants with pets, smokers, and families with children. You'll develop a natural preference on most of these areas over time, and you'll eventually find a system that works for you and fits with your wider aims and objectives.

Keys to success

Don't be fooled by the simplicity. Running a profitable buy-to-let investment is a challenge for most people, and it needs to be done with thought and care. To get this play right, you'll need to treat this endeavour as a small business in its own right. Here are some of the other keys to success for this particular play.

1. The investment should be ready to go – For a basic buy-to-let investment, the property should need little or no work and be ready to let out right away.
2. Pick an area with strong demand – Ignoring tenant demand is a mistake you only make once. Make sure tenant demand is strong where you're buying.
3. It should generate cash flow – Make sure there's enough margin for safety in your cash flow that it will still be positive if things go wrong.

Finally, I wanted to point out that we've used a lot of numbers and terminology in this section, some of which might be unfamiliar to the new property investor. If you need to brush up on your property numbers, I've written a separate book entirely on this topic. It's called *Essential Property Investment Calculations* and it's a crash course in all the calculations and metrics you need to know to assess a property deal and to manage a property portfolio. The book is available to buy on Amazon, and I promise that's the end of the shameless self-promotion.

Play # 21 – The light refurbishment project

Many investors build a property portfolio as a replacement for their pension and to supplement their income in retirement. This was John's main goal too – his aim was to generate an income of £1,000 per month (£12,000 per year) from his portfolio to supplement his state pension. Using basic buy-to-lets and assuming an ROI of 6%, John would need to save and invest £200,000 over the next ten years to achieve this. However, if he took on a few light refurb projects and managed to push that ROI up to 8% or so, he would only need to save £150,000 to hit that target, which seemed a lot more do-able.

Broaden your horizons

Not all properties will be the ready-to-go kind of investments we considered in our last play – some will require a bit of work first. This particular play is all about finding properties which need a bit of love, giving them a makeover, then letting them out like you would any other buy-to-let. If you add the light refurbishment project to your repertoire, you'll increase the number of deals on the market you're able to consider, increase your chances of striking a better deal, and make your investment approach more resilient.

With this play, we're talking about buying a property that needs some work, but we're not talking about gutting a property completely and taking things back to the shell. At the lighter end of the spectrum, this could be a project like putting in some new flooring and redecorating the property; at the heavier end, it could mean a new kitchen or bathroom, new flooring and carpets, replacing windows and doors, and some redecoration. This play has two main aims:

1. Striking a better deal – The returns you generate are largely a function of the price you pay for the property. The fact that the property needs some work will put some people off, increasing your chances of striking a good deal.
2. Improve your ROI – If the extra rent you can charge potential tenants after doing the work is high relative to the cost of the works, then the refurb can improve your ROI and help you achieve your goals faster.

With this play, it's all about finding the sweet spot. If the property only needs a lick of paint, it's unlikely to put off potential buyers; at the same time, however, you're not looking for a complete wreck. You're looking for a property that needs just a little bit more work than most people are prepared to do, and you're trying to use this fact to help you strike a better deal.

A worked example

We're going to build off the example we considered in the last play and look at how a light refurb could impact on the ROI we achieve. Just to recap briefly, the property we considered was a two-bedroom, two-bathroom apartment close to Leeds City Centre. We estimated that if we managed to secure the flat for around the £160,000 mark, we might achieve an ROI close to 5.0% p.a. and a positive cash flow of around £208 per month.

The figures above assume we spent no money refurbishing the property and that we simply bought it and let it out in its current state. But suppose the property was actually a little bit run down and that it could benefit from a light refurbishment consisting of the following works: (a) a new kitchen, including a replacement of the electrical appliances; (b) a new bathroom and a new ensuite; (c) replacement of the laminate wooden flooring in the hallway and lounge and new carpets in the bedrooms; (d) a redecoration throughout, including painting all the walls and ceiling; (e) new fixtures and fittings like lamp shades and some uplighting, which would give the apartment a more modern and high-end feel. Suppose we estimate that in total these works could cost around £10,000 to complete; we also believe that after completing the works, the property could let out for an increased rent of £900 per month, a £75 increase versus our base case where we carried out no refurbishment. The numbers then work out as follows.

	No refurb	With refurb
Expected income		
Rental income	£825	£900
Monthly expenditure	£617	£617
Profit / (loss)	£208	£283
Cash invested		
– Deposit (25% × £160,000)	£40,000	£40,000
– Stamp duty	£5,500	£5,500
– Furnishing costs	£2,000	£2,000
– Valuation and survey	£500	£500
– Legal expenses	£1,500	£1,500
– Mortgage broker	£500	£500
– Refurbishment costs	-	£10,000
Total cash invested	£50,000	£60,000

In the right-hand column, I've shown how the figures could look after the light refurb is carried out. That is, we expect to achieve £900 of rental income versus our monthly expenses of £617. We could expect to generate £283 of cash flow each month or around £3,396 of annual pre-tax profit. To see what this gives us as an ROI, we take the annual profit of £3,396 ÷ £60,000 (i.e. the money we put into the deal, including the £10,000 refurbishment costs) which is an annual ROI of 5.7% before tax.

In this example, the ROI of 5.7% after the refurbishment is higher than the ROI of 5.0% with no refurbishment, and it tells us that we're better off if we complete the refurb project. If the results were the other way around, i.e. if the ROI was lower after the refurbishment, then you may consider not doing the project at all or you may think about how you could lower the refurb costs, e.g. by lowering the specification to make the project itself more profitable.

Keys to success

As with any property investment strategy, the key to pulling off a successful light refurb is to make sure that you do everything you can to accurately estimate the costs involved and then manage the project carefully through to completion. Here are just a few of the areas you'll need to think about before starting.

Getting the right team in place

Unless you work in the building trade, getting the right team in place to carry out the works is going to be key. Depending on the project you're undertaking, you may need any or all of the following: a builder, an electrician, a plumber, a painter or decorator, and a general handyman. Other specialists, e.g. flooring experts, window and door fitters, tilers for bathroom and kitchen works, can often be arranged via other tradespeople and can be brought in to do specific jobs.

If you don't have contacts yourself, you could try reaching out to your network for a personal recommendation. Failing that, you might try appointing a letting agent to manage the property for you once the works have been completed on the proviso that they'll share their contacts in the building trade with you and help you get access to the tradespeople you need. This can be particularly helpful if you're new to a city and you need to expand your local network. As a last resort, you could consider posting a job on one of the tradespeople websites.

Drawing up a schedule of works

You'll want to draw up a schedule of the works, including a list of specifications, and cost out each element before you put in your offer for the property. If you have a strong network and can arrange for your builder to view the property with you that's even better. Your builder will be able to give you a quote and you'll be able to lock in the price before you do the deal. If you're going it alone in the initial buying phase, call some tradespeople and ask them for indicative quotes, then add on a margin for prudence in their estimates.

For all but the lightest of refurb projects, you'll want to get a written quote for the works to be completed. The quote should provide a granular breakdown of all the tasks to be completed, and it should provide an estimate of the costs, split between labour, materials and the cost of any agreed upon items, e.g. a bathroom suite, set of kitchen units, or a specific type of flooring. It should also detail the expected project timescales, who will carry out the works, and set out a point of contact for day-to-day delivery of the services.

For bigger jobs, you may want to get in place some kind of simple contract which covers all of the above and sets out some provisions around what happens if things go wrong. The Federation of Master Builders has put together a template that you can print off from their website and fill in the blanks.

Ensuring compliance with regulations

When undertaking any property refurbishment project, it's important to know whether the works will need approval in terms of building regulations, planning permission, or both. In general, the bigger projects like home extensions and loft conversions, will require planning permission, as will anything which requires a change of use. However, certain other types of work also require approval from the building regulations department of the local authority. You should speak to your tradespeople about this to make sure you understand which works need approval, the process for certifying the completed works, and to obtain copies of any documentation or certificates you might need later.

You can find information on building regulations, including a list of common projects that require approval, on the Government's planning portal. If you're new to refurbs, make sure to educate yourself on this before you start.

Strong project management

Given this is a light refurb project and it's likely to be at the less complicated end of the spectrum, you might be tempted to oversee the works yourself. This means you'll be hiring in individual tradespeople yourself and coordinating the project. In general, I wouldn't recommend this for first-time refurbers, unless you have previous building experience, as you need to have a good working knowledge of the construction process to ensure things run smoothly and on time. If this is an area you're looking to improve your skills, why not hire one main contractor to serve as a project manager and then shadow them on a couple of jobs.

It's also worth pointing out that if you're investing remotely, e.g. buying in the north, but living in the south, you'll almost certainly want to delegate the project management to a professional. The extra challenge in this case is keeping in touch with the progress of the works and being there to make any decisions you need to make. Try to find a builder who's prepared to Skype or Facetime you daily or weekly to walk you through the progress and highlight any decisions needed – that way, you can keep the site visits to a minimum.

Marketing the property early

Just because the property looks like a building site, it doesn't mean you can't be marketing it out. Once the site is safe, you should start marketing the property or asking your letting agent to promote the property to prospective tenants. Your aim here is to minimise any void period and start generating income as soon as the property is ready to let out. If tenants are having a hard time imagining the property in its end state, you could consider offering a discount in the form of a couple of weeks rent-free at the start of the tenancy. Overall, that may work out cheaper than a long void period.

The golden rule of refurbs

Before we move on to our next play, let's finish with a couple of my golden rules of property refurbishments.

Golden rule # 1

Golden rule # 1 is that you absolutely have to build in a contingency fund. Adding 10% to 15% to the estimated cost of the works will protect you from all kinds of problems and will reduce the stress of the project no-end. Without one, you'll be worrying about every last overrun and delay, and you likely won't sleep properly until the project is over and your new tenant has moved in.

Golden rule # 2

Golden rule # 2 is that you have to make sure you have time available for a project like this. If this is your first refurb, you'll need to manage it carefully and dedicate the time needed to get the project across the line safely. Over time as your skills and experience develop and as you build a team around you, this can get easier, but you don't want to botch your first refurb.

An inconvenient truth

Even if these kinds of projects aren't your thing, you should seriously consider developing your expertise in this area. Yes, refurbs can be hard and stressful and they're not everyone's cup of tea, but they can unlock serious value and some of the most profitable opportunities out there involve some kind of dirty work or problem to be solved. Don't let a lack of experience put you off – start small and build your experience gradually. The light refurbishment is a tool every property investor needs in their toolbox. You never know, you might even acquire a taste for this kind of project over time.

Play # 22 – How to use equity in your own home

Kim's first foray into property worked out rather fortuitously. She'd started a nursing job in 2008 in the middle of the last financial crisis, and two years' later she bought her first home, a one-bed flat in New Cross in South East London. Her timing could not have been better, though she never planned it that way. In recent years, the London market had gone nuts, and her little one-bed flat was now valued at £280,000, double what she paid for it in 2010. What's more, she only had £90,000 left on her mortgage, giving her £190,000 of equity. The only real question was how to use it.

How does it work?

If you bought a home a number of years ago or if you inherited a property from a relative, then you may well have accrued a decent chunk of equity you can use to finance future deals. This is a simple idea that property investors casually throw around in conversation, but how do you go about doing this and what are the keys to getting it right? We'll take a look at all this and more in play # 22.

A worked example

Assessing the equity available

This play is relatively straightforward and it's easy to execute. Let's take a look at a simple example. Let's say you and your family bought a home ten years ago for

£120,000 and used a 75% loan-to-value repayment mortgage to finance the deal at a 2% interest rate with a term of 25 years. That means you put down a deposit of £30,000 and you took out a mortgage of £90,000, which you've been paying down ever since.

Ten years and 120 mortgage payments later, the property has seen good capital growth and its market value is now estimated to be £180,000. In addition, we've been making monthly repayments against the loan, so the amount we owe has decreased from £90,000 to £60,000. Taken altogether, that means we have £180,000 – £60,000 = £120,000 of equity accrued in the property, and we can potentially use some of this to finance future deals.

Pulling out the funds

In order to pull out the cash to invest, we'll need to remortgage. Building off the example above, suppose we decided to remortgage the property based on the valuation of £180,000 and using a new 75% loan-to-value mortgage. Then we would leave 25% × £180,000 = £45,000 of equity in the property, and we would take out a new loan of 75% × £180,000 = £135,000. We would then repay the original mortgage provider the £60,000 outstanding loan balance, leaving us with £75,000 of cash in our bank account to invest in new property deals.

The impact of the remortgage

That's the easy bit over with. The harder part is understanding whether it makes good financial sense to use the equity we've accrued in this way. To understand this, we'll need to do a few more calculations.

When we went through the remortgage, we increased our outstanding loan from £60,000 to £135,000, that is we borrowed an additional £75,000. As a result, our mortgage payments will increase. You can use your favourite online mortgage calculator to check the following figures are correct (I use the one at www.moneysavingexpert.com/mortgages/mortgage-rate-calculator) but the refinance will increase your mortgage payments from £382 per month to £572 per month, assuming we are still able to secure a 2% interest rate (the same as the original loan) and that we re-spread the £135,000 loan amount after the remortgage over a new 25 year mortgage term starting at the refinance date. That is, our monthly mortgage payments will increase by £190.

Let's take a look at the other side of the coin, i.e. what we're going to do with the money raised. Well, if we invest the £75,000 of cash raised in buy-to-let deals that generate an ROI of 6%, then your new investments will generate 6% × £75,000 = £4,500 per year or £375 per month before tax. Overall, we've been able to improve our cash flow by £375 – £190 = £185 per month, before we take tax into account. In addition, because we've taken out a new repayment mortgage, we'll again be building up equity in our home afterwards.

Finally, it's also worth noting that by using the equity in our own home in this way, we've also been able to expand the size of our property portfolio. Before the remortgage, we owned one property worth £180,000; afterwards, we might own additional properties worth £75,000 ÷ 0.25 = £300,000 (if we bought the extra buy-to-let properties using a 75% loan-to-value mortgage) and the total value of our portfolio is now £480,000. We're more leveraged, of course, but this increase in the size of our portfolio positions us nicely if property prices continue to rise in the future and could seriously increase our net worth longer term.

Keys to success

As with all of these strategies, there are things you need to do to get it right. Here are a few of the keys to success for this play:

- Make sure your partner is onboard – Anything to do with your own home has the potential to be emotive. You should make sure your partner is onboard with this play and understands the benefits it can bring. If they're struggling with the concept, you could always consider taking out less equity.
- Getting confident with the numbers – The figures we looked at above worked because the ROI we were projecting was high enough to justify the play. To

make this worthwhile, you need to get confident that the ROI you can achieve is significantly in excess of the interest rate on your mortgage.

- Getting comfortable with debt – This play only works if you're comfortable taking on extra debt and increasing your leverage. It's best to avoid this play in the latter stages of the property cycle, as the ROI on new investments will likely be low at this stage in the cycle.

- Use a good mortgage broker – I would always recommend using a mortgage broker when you're refinancing any deal, but they can be particularly useful with this strategy. They can help you get the best rate and explore the impact on your monthly cash flow of various loan-to-value options.

- Watch out for early repayment charges – When you remortgage with a new provider (as opposed to a product transfer with your existing lender) you're using the new loan to pay off the previous lender. If you're still in your fixed-rate period, you should watch out for any early repayment charges.

Reversal

There are times in life when this play is not the right one for some people. If you're later in life and your children have flown the nest, you may be better off selling the property, locking in those gains, and then downsizing your home. With new mortgage products coming on to the market all the time for those later in life, you might still be able to get a mortgage on your new home purchase, and it could unlock even more funds to plough back into future investments.

Likewise, if you've got a young family and might soon need a bigger place, you may want to use the equity you've accrued as a deposit on a new home instead. Although the cold calculated, numbers-driven investor in me is at pains to admit it, there are times in life when other things are more important than making an optimal investment decision. Starting a new family and bringing children into the world are certainly amongst them.

Play # 23 – How to use a second mortgage charge

The townhouse Greg bought in Salford three years ago had soared in value along with other Manchester property. Working in the building trade, he saw the Manchester boom coming and bought in early – his reward was £50,000 of extra equity in his home. Greg's problem was he'd taken out a five-year mortgage with early repayment charges, so he couldn't use this right away.

A first look at second mortgages

When most people purchase a home, they take out a loan from a lender who uses the property they've purchased as collateral. This home loan is called a mortgage, or more specifically, a *first mortgage*. The borrower is typically required to repay the loan plus interest each month, and over time the borrower builds up equity in the property through their repayments and any price increases.

After a few years, a homeowner may decide to borrow against equity they've accrued in the property to fund projects or other expenditures. The loan they take out against their accrued equity is known as a *second mortgage*, as the borrower has left the first mortgage in place. A second mortgage charge, sometimes known as a *home equity loan*, is a kind of second mortgage made while the first mortgage is still in effect. The homeowner receives a cash sum, the loan amount, from the lender and signs up to repay the loan over a specified term at a particular rate of interest, just like for a first mortgage.

In the event of a default, the first mortgage provider repossesses the property and receives all the proceeds from the liquidation until the first mortgage is paid off. The second mortgage provider receives whatever is left from the proceeds of the sale. Because the second mortgage provider receives repayments only when the first mortgage is paid back, second mortgages are riskier for the lender. As such, the interest rate charged for a second mortgage is usually higher and the amount borrowed is usually lower than for the first mortgage.

Why take out a second mortgage

For those with accrued equity in their own homes, second mortgage charges can be a great way to raise additional capital for investment. Second charges can often be arranged quickly, without affecting the first mortgage. As such, they can be ideal for customers who want to protect an existing mortgage. This might be the case, for example, if you enjoy a low mortgage interest rate that's better than anything currently offered in the market; or perhaps you're on an interest only mortgage and you wouldn't be eligible for this on a remortgage, due to a change in lending criteria or your personal circumstances.

There are other situations where second mortgage charges can come in handy as a financing option. Say you're struggling to get access to some form of personal loan, e.g. if you're self-employed, a second mortgage might offer a way to help you secure the funds you need. Likewise, if your first mortgage has early repayment charges and if you're locked into a fixed-rate period, then it might be cheaper for you to take out a second mortgage, rather than do a remortgage. These kinds of situations are actually pretty common.

How to use the funds

This play is more about how to raise the funds you need, not how to use them. As with a remortgage, you're free to use the capital you raise however you like. For some people, this could mean putting the cash to use in buy-to-let investments, and we covered the details of this in our last play. You could also use the cash sum raised as a pool of starter capital to finance property flips or in place of a personal loan to finance a home extension project.

It's also worth pointing out that you could potentially use the funds to help a child get onto the property ladder. Say your daughter was just starting out in a job and was keen to put play # 18, the young professional landlord (or should I say landlady), into action. You could take out a second mortgage charge on your own home equal to the amount she needs for that deposit, with the rest of the monies needed for the purchase coming from a traditional homeowner mortgage secured on the property itself. This strategy offers a way to finance 100% of the purchase, no savings needed. Your daughter would, however, need to factor the higher repayments needed into her cash flow projections.

Reversal

If you only need to raise a small amount money, you're generally better off going for an unsecured product such as a personal loan. Like first mortgages, there are costs associated with taking out a second mortgage. These include valuation fees, legal fees and the cost of using a broker, if you decide to use one. So, with the cost of arranging a second mortgage potentially running to £1,000 or more, it's not worth it if you're only looking to raise a small amount of cash.

If you don't have a large early repayment charge on your mortgage, if you have a decent amount of equity in your home, and if your personal circumstances have not changed, you'll likely be better off remortgaging or speaking to your current mortgage provider to see if they could offer a further advance. Second mortgages are, after all, just another tool in the property investor's toolkit and one that won't be useful in all circumstances.

Play # 24 – Try your luck with seller financing

While trawling through Rightmove listings in her usual property hotspots, Nicole stumbled across a spacious two-bedroom flat that would work well as a buy-to-let for young professionals. The listing was for cash-only buyers, owing to cladding issues rendering the flat unmortgageable. She had half of the money she needed for the deal, but she'd need to find a way to raise the rest. What if there was a way she could buy the property and find a way to finance the purchase that wasn't via the traditional mortgage route?

A little-known secret

Most property books that promise secret techniques and fast results are just overhyped promotional materials trying to sell some course or another. At the risk of sounding a little too salesy myself, our next play is about one of the lesser known areas of property investment – seller financing. I'd go as far as saying that most property investors have never heard of it. But like all the plays we've looked at so far, there's a time and a place for seller financing.

When it comes to financing residential property purchases, most transactions follow a well-trodden path. The seller finds a buyer – either an owner-occupier with the required level of income, employment history, and credit score to qualify for a mortgage or a property investor with a strong track record and a large enough deposit to meet the lender's rental stress test calculations – and the lender puts up the bulk of the money needed to finance the deal. But what if traditional financing is unavailable and the buyer and seller still want to proceed? Enter what's known as seller financing.

What is seller financing?

As the term implies, the person who's selling the property is also the person who finances the purchase – there is no bank, mortgage provider or lender involved. The buyer and seller make the arrangements themselves. They agree on the price to be paid for the property, the amount that's to be paid from the buyer to the seller at completion, and a payment schedule setting out the timeframe over which the rest of the purchase price will be paid.

It's common to set out the details of the payment schedule in what's known as a *promissory note*, which specifies the term and frequency of the payments, the interest rate on the lending, and any consequences should the buyer default on those obligations. The seller's financing of the deal typically runs for a shorter period than a traditional mortgage term, say five years or less. And there's often a *balloon payment*, i.e. a larger one-off sum scheduled at the end of the repayment period. The theory, or the hope at least, is that the buyer will eventually be able to refinance the purchase with a traditional lender, having solved whatever the problem was that made the property unmortgageable.

The pros and cons

When mortgages are hard to get

As an alternative to traditional mortgages, seller financing is a useful option at times or in places where mortgages are hard to get. This could, for example, be the case where a property is made of non-standard materials or using an unusual construction method. It might also be the case for a leasehold property with a short lease or for a property in a complete state of disrepair – think no running water, no kitchen and bathroom, and a complete wreck of a property that needs serious work. In short, it's likely to be either a Homes Under the Hammer job or have some legal or other issue that's difficult to solve.

In tight circumstances like this, seller financing allows buyers to access an alternative form of credit. Sellers, in turn, can tap a population of willing buyers in a situation where it would be difficult to sell the property. Depending on the number of buyers, the seller might also be able to command a higher sale price for the property than would otherwise be the case.

Cheaper transaction costs

With only two main parties involved, seller financing can be quicker and cheaper than selling a property by the traditional method. When the seller finances the transaction, the deal usually closes faster, as there is no waiting around for the lender to carry out their valuation and for their loan officer, underwriter and legal team to clear the loan. Likewise, buyers tend to like seller financing, because they can buy the property with less money down. If this all sounds too good to be true, let's provide some balance.

The seller needs to be able to finance the deal

Seller financing is at its simplest when the seller owns the property outright. In this situation, the seller is free to sell the property and agree to payment terms they are happy with as part of the sale process.

If, however, the seller still has an outstanding mortgage on the property, this can introduce extra complications. Paying for a title search on the property will help a buyer confirm that the property is accurately described in the deed and is free from mortgages. Most mortgages have a 'due on sale' clause that prohibits the seller from selling the property without paying off the mortgage. In this situation, the seller should look to pay off the outstanding loan as part of the sale process, possibly through a combination of the part-payment received from the buyer and perhaps needing to put in some additional funds of their own.

Keys to success

The buyer's perspective

From a buyer's perspective, here are some useful tips and realities to keep in mind if you're considering using seller financing.

- Don't expect better terms than a traditional mortgage – The seller is exposed to the credit risk associated with you, the buyer, defaulting on the payment schedule. The interest rate and deposit amount may be similar to or higher than with a traditional mortgage.
- Sell yourself to the seller – The seller needs to be confident they're lending to a credible counterparty that's likely to meet their commitments. Be open and transparent about your credit history, employment, financial assets and liabilities. Offer references that demonstrate credibility.
- Be prepared to propose seller financing – When you see a situation that could lend itself to seller financing, be prepared to propose it. Not all sellers are aware this is an option, and they may be grateful to you if this helps them get a deal over the line that they're comfortable with.

The seller's perspective

There are also some useful things to be aware of from a seller's perspective. Let's take a look at some of these.

- You don't need to finance the sale for long – As the seller, you can at any time consider selling the promissory note to an investor. The buyer then sends the payments to this party instead. However, you'll likely have to accept less than the full value of the note to sell it, say 70% to 90% of its face value.
- Make it part of your sales pitch – If you've decided to offer seller financing, you should say so in your sales materials and listing. It's relatively rare to use seller financing, so you should promote the fact you're offering it and make sure you explain what it is.

- Get the right advice – You'll want to make sure the legal agreements drawn up as part of the deal are watertight and offer the buyer no wriggle room. At the same time, you should speak to a tax adviser to make sure the payment schedule works well from a tax perspective.

Both parties

Compared with the well-trodden path of a traditional property purchase, seller financing can seem complicated. Getting it right is all about the details. Both the buyer and seller should hire an experienced lawyer and you should work with an estate agent experienced in these sorts of deals to write and review the final sales contract and the promissory note. You don't want to hire just any conveyancing solicitor here; you want to work with an experienced professional who's done this kind of deal before. Good legal input will help the buyer and seller strike a fair and even deal and protect both parties against the various risks that they face in this unusual and unfamiliar type of transaction.

Play # 25 – Flipping properties for a profit

After their children had flown the nest, Suhrid and his wife were desperate to take up a new project. With decent savings in the bank and time available, they wanted to try property flipping, something they thought they'd be good at having refurbished their home a couple of times. The ultimate aim was for Suhrid to carve-out a full-time role in property and quit his job.

No reward without risk

Our next play, flipping properties for a profit, needs no introduction. This strategy is what comes to most people's minds when they think about property, probably owing to the fact that it makes for good TV. At its heart, this play is less about investment, and it's more akin to commercial ventures such as those undertaken by property developers. The premise is straightforward – buy a property, carry out a refurbishment, and sell it for a profit. There's no long-term letting involved, just the promise of cash profits for a job well done.

As we discussed in play # 21, there's a broad spectrum of projects you could undertake. At the lighter end, we're talking about redecoration, changing the floor coverings like carpets and laminates, and checking that the boiler, central heating, and the electrics are serviceable and fit-for-purpose. In the middle, we might be looking at replacing doors and windows, adding blinds and curtains, or lighter cosmetic changes to a kitchen or bathroom, e.g. new cupboard doors and handles, changing taps to give them a more modern look, etc. At the heavier end of the spectrum, we might consider projects involving a replacement kitchen or bathroom, a new boiler or central heating system, and changes to the electrics, such as moving the position of sockets or switches.

The key principle at work in any property flip is that you need to "add value" to the property. You should focus your efforts and your resources on those areas that will add the most value to the end price. Firstly, this means that you need to know your end market well and be comfortable that the money you're spending will translate into a higher sale price. Secondly, it means you're more likely to be taking on projects needing a medium or heavy refurbishment, as this is where there's more potential to add value. Don't overlook light refurbishments though, there's money to be made there too. With bigger projects, there's bigger things that can go wrong. So, if you're new to flips, start small and build your experience gradually over time. Ultimately, there's no reward without some level of risk – just make sure it's a level of risk you can handle.

A tale of two valuation methods

Two property valuation methods lie at the heart of successful property flips. The first valuation method, known as the *comparison method of valuation*, is used to estimate the final sale price of the refurbished property. The second method, the *residual method of valuation*, is the method used to estimate the price that you're prepared to pay for the property before any of the works have been completed. Let's take a closer look at these two valuation methods.

The comparison method of valuation

Of these two methods, this is the most straightforward. It relies on an analysis of similar transactions to give us an estimate of a property's market value, i.e. the estimated sale price for the property. The method is simple and transparent, but it does have its limitations. For example, some properties do not have any direct comparables, perhaps owing to their location or unique characteristics.

With this method, we analyse recent sold prices for similar transactions in the market. It tends to work best where there are regular transactions happening in the local market and where there are properties similar in nature. The first step is to collect the raw data we need on comparables. These days, data is available from a range of sources, including the online portals like Rightmove and Zoopla and from HM Land Registry. The data you collect should be for similar properties that are close by and that have sold recently.

Once we've collected the basic data, we need to consider any adjustments that might be needed. For example, if one of our comparables has a floor space 10% bigger than the property we're valuing, we should consider knocking 10% off the sold price of the comparable to account for its larger size. We could also consider adjusting for things like aspect, or the specific position of a property within a block, the number of rooms, provided we don't double count this versus usable floor space, the availability of parking, and the condition of the property. Other factors could include the size of the garden, standard of décor, condition of the central heating system, the presence of double glazing, and many other things we haven't listed here.

Remember that with flips, we're trying to estimate the final sale price, so we should do this on a *look through basis* – that is, we're trying to estimate its value once all the refurbishment works have been completed, so the comparables we use should be relevant for this. Once we've adjusted the raw data, we can take a simple average of the sale prices for the comparables then adjust it – upwards or downwards – in line with any other factors. There's an element of subjectivity in any estimate, and the better you know the local market, the better you'll be able to estimate the market value after the works are complete. To help you with this, you could also check your figures with a trusted adviser in your property team, like a local estate agent that you trust or even your accountant. The final estimate, however, should be all your own. If you're in any doubt, make sure you err on the side of caution, as you don't want to overestimate the final sale price and put your profits at risk.

The residual method of valuation

The residual method of valuation is most frequently used by property developers to estimate the price they're prepared to pay for a piece of land they intend to develop. To do this, they estimate the final value of a completed development and subtract off the cost of the development and their profit margin to arrive at a *residual land value* – that is, the price they're prepared to pay for the land.

The average investor is unlikely to be taking on large development projects. However, we can use the same approach to work out the price we're prepared to pay for a property we intend to flip. The basic process for the residual method of valuation works as follows:

1. Estimated net sale price of the property

- Our estimate of the final sale price after all the works are complete
- Less any costs associated with the sale, e.g. legal fees, estate agent fees

2. Less the cost of carrying out the development

- Costs should include all the materials, labour, project management costs
- Include any financing costs, e.g. loan interest, arrangement fees, etc
- Build in your profit margin as your reward for undertaking the project
- Include all ancillary purchase costs, e.g. stamp duty, legal fees, broker fees

3. Equals the price we should pay for the property

So, the method sounds straightforward, but there's lots that can go wrong at each stage of the estimation process. As such, this method is prone to error, and it can give a wide range of answers, depending on the various assumptions and cost estimates made.

To estimate the cost of the refurbishment, you could ask for quotes from a builder in advance of purchasing the property. You can also speak to local agents and tradespeople about the potential cost of the project or some of the individual elements. If you're looking to get a rough feel for the likely cost to see if the project is even viable to begin with, you could estimate these yourself using a *schedule of works*. This is simply an itemised list of all the materials needed and works required to finish the project, i.e. a bottom-up estimate of the costs involved. You can then verify this figure with a couple of local builders.

This is where you should build in a contingency to allow for potential errors in your estimation process. For example, you could include a contingency of 10% of the total estimated cost, to guard against overruns.

If you're using a bridging loan to finance the purchase, you should include this cost in your estimates. We'll come back to this shortly, but the important thing here is to be prudent in your estimate of how many weeks or months it will take to complete the project, as you don't want to underestimate the financing costs involved. You should also include a profit margin as your reward for the time, energy and capital cost of the project. Developers use different approaches here, but the approach I like to use is to calculate the profit as a % of the final sale price. This could, for example, be anywhere in the range 5% to 15% of the final sale price, with the 5% being for a light refurb and 15% for a heavier refurb.

A worked example

To understand how this works in a bit more detail, it's useful to take a look at an example. Let's take a look at the price we'd need to pay to successfully flip a three-bedroom family home in the North West of England in a town outside of Preston. In the table, I've prepared some calculations, based on the following assumptions: (a) an estimated sale price of £250,000 less a 1.5% sales commission and legal fees of £1,250; (b) a medium refurbishment with an estimated cost of £25,000 and a building works contingency of 10% or £2,500; (c) financing costs of £9,375, if we use a bridging loan to finance the purchase instead of mortgage or nil for a cash purchase; (d) a target profit of 10% of the final sale price, consistent with a medium refurbishment project; (e) an estimated time of five months to complete the works, which impacts the financing costs.

Financing method	Bridging	Cash purchase
Final sale price	£250,000	£250,000
Sales commission (1.5% × 250,000)	(£3,750)	(£3,750)
Legal expenses	(£1,250)	(£1,250)
Estimated net sale proceeds (A)	£245,000	£245,000
Cost of the building works	£25,000	£25,000
Building works contingency (10%)	£2,500	£2,500
Financing cost (see later for breakdown)	£9,375	-
Total development costs (B)	£36,875	£27,500
Property purchase price	£175,000	£184,000
Stamp duty (including surcharge)	£6,250	£6,700
Fees (e.g. valuation, survey, legal)	£3,000	£3,000
Total purchase costs (C)	£184,250	£193,700
Estimated profit (A) – (B) – (C)	£23,875	£23,800
Cash needed to fund the deal	£89,875	£221,200

In this example, I've adjusted the property purchase price up or down as needed, including the knock-on impact on the stamp duty cost, until the estimated profit is around 10% of the net sale proceeds or close to £24,000. In this example, we can afford to pay £175,000 for the property and make £23,875 estimated profit, if we use a bridging loan to fund the purchase. If we go down the cash purchase route, rather than using bridging finance, we can afford to pay £184,000 and still make a £23,800 estimated profit.

Let's take a closer look at the cost of the building works. We've estimated the cost of the works as follows: £11,000 to fit a new kitchen, bathroom and ensuite shower; £2,500 for a boiler; £5,000 to fit new double glazed windows and replace external doors at the front and back of the property; £2,500 for new carpets in all the bedrooms, laminate floorings in the lounge, kitchen and hallways, and new vinyl floorings in the bathrooms; £3,000 for the cost of redecoration throughout; £1,000 for some general clean up and painting the exterior of the property.

Finally, it's worth a comment on the cash needed. With the cash purchase, this is a large sum of around £221,200, which includes £184,000 to buy the property, £9,700 to cover stamp duty and fees, and £27,500 for the total development costs. With bridging finance, we need a smaller sum of around £89,875, which includes £43,750 for the deposit (£175,000 × 25% assuming an LTV of 75%) to buy the property, £9,250 to cover stamp duty and fees, and £36,875 for the development costs, including the £9,375 in financing costs.

Sensitivity analysis

The outcome of the process above can be susceptible to changes in the variables, including the development costs, financing costs, delays and project overruns. I recommend using some sort of sensitivity analysis to show how your profit might change as the key variables in your residual valuation change. For example, the table below shows how your profit changes assuming a +/- 20 per cent change in development costs and a +/- 5% change in the final sale price. The figures shown below are for the scenario where we use a bridging loan to finance the deal.

Development costs	Final sale price		
	-5%	No change	+5%
+20%	£6,063	£18,375	£30,688
No change	£11,563	£23,875	£36,188
-20%	£17,063	£29,375	£41,688

Based on this sensitivity analysis, we can see our estimated profit could be as low as £6,063 (if the final sale price achieved was 5% lower than our estimate and if development costs were 20% higher) or as high as £41,688 (if we achieved a 5%

higher sale price than expected and if our development costs were 20% lower than expected). This kind of sensitivity analysis can be useful for "book-ending" the range of outcomes and making sure our project is likely to be profitable even if a couple of the key variables go against us.

If you're going to use this method in your flips and refurb projects, then do make sure you're adding in enough of a contingency to avoid a loss. Also, do make sure you get input from experienced developers and tradespeople, if you can, to increase the accuracy of your estimates. This is likely to be particularly important in your first few developments or if you're taking on a project outside of your comfort zone to stretch yourself. In short, don't be afraid to use other people's experience to supplement your own to help you get a better outcome.

An aside on bridging finance

In our example above, we considered the amount of cash you'd need to fund the project if you carried this out with bridging finance and as a cash purchase. The amount needed for the cash-only deal is high, which will rule out this option for most investors. At the same time, however, using a mortgage (which is essentially a long-term financing product for buy-and-hold investors) to carry out a flip is not good practice, and it could get you into a bit of hot water if you do this one too many times.

The alternative is to use bridging finance. You can think of bridging finance as a kind of short-term mortgage. Like a mortgage, the amount the lender will lend to you is determined by the value of the property, and they'll take a charge over the property as security. In addition, you'll pay interest for the agreed loan term, then pay back the loan at the end. Unlike a mortgage, bridging finance is a much shorter duration product, with typical loan terms being 12 months or less. Also, bridging finance tends to be a lot more expensive, with annualised interest rates on the borrowing being anywhere between 8% and 15%, and there are other fees and costs involved too.

So, if bridging finance is a lot more expensive, why would you consider using it? Here are a few of the key reasons:

- When the hold period is short – The expected timescale for most flips is short, so bridging finance is the ideal candidate, whether you ultimately plan to sell the property for profit or remortgage it later.
- If speed matters – You can arrange bridging finance in weeks, not months. This allows you to compete with cash buyers in situations where you can get a good deal by moving quickly, e.g. auctions or repossessions.
- Where the property isn't mortgageable – If the property isn't habitable, then you're unlikely to be able to get a mortgage. Bridging finance, however, can still be used, even if you want to flip a property that's a bit of a wreck.

In terms of how much you could borrow, this is similar to a buy-to-let mortgage. Lenders might be prepared to offer you up to say 70% or 75% of the property's current market value. Some lenders will offer loans against the *gross development value* – that is, what the property will be worth once you've completed the works. In that case, you may be able to borrow some of the cash needed to complete the development works, allowing you to take on bigger projects. If you're interested in finding out more, you should speak to a good broker about your options.

The fees you pay tend to vary between lenders. Here's a quick overview of the kinds of costs you'll incur, along with the estimated cost for the worked example shown a few pages ago:

- the initial valuation fee, e.g. I've assumed £500 in the example
- arrangement fee of 1%-2% of the loan, e.g. 1% × 75% × £175,000 = £1,312
- interest costs, e.g. 1% per month × 5 months × 75% × £175,000 = £6,563
- the lender's legal fees, e.g. assumed to be £1,000 here

In this example, the fees and charges above come to £9,375 as the total cost of the bridging finance, but in practice there could be other charges on top of this. Some lenders charge exit fees, which might be about 1% of the amount borrowed. Also, if you arrange the loan through a broker, the broker fee could be up to 1% of the loan amount. So, it isn't cheap, but it can give you access to deals you don't have the cash savings for yourself.

There are two important things to bear in mind when you're using bridging finance. Firstly, you need to make sure that the costs are fully factored into your model, and that the project will still produce the desired level of profitability after factoring in all borrowing costs. Secondly, you need to be confident that you have a good exit strategy, e.g. whether that be a sale or a remortgage, and that you can execute it within the loan term. Make sure that the loan term is long enough, as it can be expensive to try to extend it.

Selling the property

Once the refurbishment is complete, it's time to get your property on the market and turn all that hard work into some profit. You'll want the property to appeal to the largest possible number of buyers, so it's definitely worth spending some time and effort presenting it in the best light you can. You want to appeal to the owner-occupier market, as you want someone (ideally more than one person) to fall in love with the property and bid with their heart, not their head. That's the way to generate an even bigger profit. You should consider getting professional photos taken – a small, one-off cost relative to the big prize at stake. In addition, you could consider "staging" the property with furniture that's rented-in to show the property off at its best and paint a picture of what life could look like if your buyer lived there. This can make a big difference to the end price, and it's not a step many investors take. Finally, once you've struck a deal with a buyer, make sure you put some pressure on your solicitor to keep things moving, as this can mean money in your account weeks earlier and, if you're using bridging finance, lower financing costs and higher profits for the venture.

Keys to success

We've covered some of the keys to success as we've gone through the details of this play and in play # 21. To wrap this up, here's a roundup of my top tips, with a couple of new ones thrown in for good measure.

- Be conservative with your estimates – I've said this a number of times above, but being conservative with your figures will save you from many mistakes.
- Tailor your product for the target market – Have a target buyer in mind, e.g. a young family or retired couple, and tailor the works for this market.
- Consider a range of scenarios – You should model a light, medium and heavy refurb scenario in your figures and see which one gives the most profit.
- Build up your experience gradually – If you're new to flips, start small and build your experience and your network of contacts gradually.
- Flip where the flipping is best – You don't need to stick to properties or areas that would be good for buy-to-let. The world is your oyster.

And finally, it's also worth pointing out that many property investors partner this play with the basic buy-to-let. Suppose, for example, you had £100,000 to invest, but you wanted to build a portfolio of say 10 to 20 properties as quickly as you can. Well, rather than investing the £100,000 in two buy-to-let properties and then starting to save again from scratch, some investors use this £100,000 to flip properties instead, e.g. say by doing two flips of the kind we looked at above to generate £50,000 in profit. They could then invest this £50,000 profit in a basic buy-to-let, leaving their £100,000 still in the bank. If you executed this strategy once a year, you could buy one buy-to-let property per year all off the same initial savings pot of £100,000 without saving another dime. It's a great idea, and it's perfect for investors with time on their hands, but less ability to save.

Play # 26 – Partner up for a flip (JV strategy # 1)

Helen worked in a property auction house and her boyfriend Matt worked in the building trade – in fact, that's how they met. With Helen's access to deals and Matt's experience in construction, they were ideally placed to spot and execute flips, but they lacked the resources to take advantage of every good deal that crossed their path. Helen wondered if some kind of joint venture with a hands-off financial backer might be the ideal way to capitalise on these extra opportunities.

The power of joint ventures

Our next play, which I've called partner up for a flip, is the first of our joint venture (or "JV") strategies. Joint ventures are commonly touted by property guru types as the cure to almost every property ailment – from having no money to invest to having no experience. And although they can be a great way to work when two or more parties are each bringing something to the deal, they can, if they're not properly structured, be a quick way to lose money and your reputation.

In this section, we're going to take a general look at joint ventures, then we're going to move on to talk about the most common kind of JV – partnering up for a flip. We'll talk about the ins and outs of this type of project and the steps you need to take to get it right. There's a lot involved in setting up a joint venture, whether that be a property JV or any other kind of venture where two parties are working together. There's finding the right partner, deciding how it will work, agreeing on a deal structure that protects all parties involved, and then drawing up some kind of written agreement to document it all. That's before the project has even begun. I'll do my best to cover all this and more in play # 26.

A short introduction to JVs

Despite all the caveats above, joint ventures can be a great way to get started in property. They can help you get started sooner, and they can be a great way to share resources, knowledge, and experience.

Keeping things simple, a joint venture is any situation where two or more parties come together to work on a project jointly. The parties will combine the various resources, skills and know-how at their disposal to take on a commercial venture of some kind. This kind of venture is super common in the wider business world, and things are no different in the world of property.

The key to a successful property JV is finding the right marriage of skills and resources to make the project work, each party needing what the other has to offer, but at the same time bringing something to the table themselves. It's easy to imagine how a joint venture might work between say a rich uncle with financial resources at his disposal and his nephew who works in the construction trade. In reality, there are all kinds of joint ventures that could make sense, depending on the unique skillsets and experience of the parties involved. However, there are three main reasons people look to joint ventures:

1. Access to finance – People often look at JVs when they've run out of cash. For example, you might have spotted a promising flip project, but you don't have the money to buy the property or pay for the refurb. In this case, you could look to a JV partner with spare funds for financial backing.
2. Access to skills or knowledge – Another reason people look at JVs is to access a skillset they don't possess. For example, you might have the money to carry out a project, but you might feel you lack the necessary skills and experience,

e.g. construction skills, to execute the project successfully. Alternatively, you might be hampered by time constraints.

3. To align commercial interests – Finally, you might consider a JV for a large project where it's important to align the interests of all parties. For example, it might be your preference that, on a large construction project, the architect and builder you're working with have some "skin in the game", e.g. via an equity stake or otherwise.

It goes without saying that one of the keys to success with joint ventures is to find the right JV partner, and we'll come back to this point shortly. Firstly, however, let's look at how a property flip works from a JV perspective.

What the flip?

Flipping a property for a profit, that is buying a property, carrying out a refurb, and then selling the property, is by far the most common form of joint venture. The general situation is simple: one partner has the financial resources to back the project; the other partner has the time and experience to carry out the works. It could also be the case that each is providing some of the financial backing, but the project is too large for either of them to execute it alone.

The project is a simple property flip, and since we've covered flips in detail in play # 25, I won't cover that again here, as the same considerations will apply. What's new here, is that we'll need to think about how we structure the JV and the flip from a risk and reward perspective. There are two main options.

As a profit share

This type of structure is what most people have in mind when you talk about joint ventures. In simple terms, the profit made through the venture, i.e. the property flip, is split between parties in some pre-agreed way. Using a simplified version of the figures I presented in play # 25, suppose the property flip is carried out by two parties using bridging finance and that the figures work out as follows:

- the total purchase cost for the property is £185,000
- total development costs, including bridging finance are £35,000
- the net sale price after all selling expenses is £245,000

In this example, the total pre-tax profit for the flip is £25,000, and the two parties might have agreed in advance to share the profits 50:50. So, each of the parties walks away from the venture with £12,500 of profit.

This kind of 50:50 set-up might be okay if the two parties are equally involved in the financing and the day-to-day delivery. It might also work well if one party is providing the financing and the other party finds the deal, manages the project, and does the work. The important thing is that both parties are happy with the structure and that the terms are clear to everyone. It's also possible to vary the profit split, e.g. say 60:40 or 70:30, depending on the financial resources, time, and expertise each party is bringing to the table.

As a financing agreement

An alternative way to structure a JV where one party is providing the financing and the other is doing the work is for the financial backer to charge a fixed rate of interest on their capital, rather than take a percentage of the final profits. Let's use a simplified version of the figures in play # 25, but for the cash purchase.

- the total purchase cost for the property is £195,000
- the total development costs are £25,000
- the net sale proceeds after all selling expenses is £245,000

In this example, the total pre-tax profit for the flip is £25,000. The party providing the finance has agreed a fixed interest rate of 1% per month on the capital they've provided. In total, they've injected £220,000, so if the project took five months to complete, the party doing the work would owe the finance provider interest calculated as £220,000 × 1% × 5 months, which equals £11,000. The party doing the work would then deduct the £11,000 from the £25,000 total profit they've made, and they'd be left with £14,000 for their hard work.

The important difference in this second set-up versus the profit share is who's taking on the risk if things go wrong. With the profit share, if costs overrun or if the timescales get delayed, both parties share in the downside; they also share in the upside if things go well. However, structuring the joint venture as a financing arrangement instead means that the party doing all the work is also bearing all the risk: if the project overruns on costs or if timescales get delayed, the financing partner still makes their 1% per month, and the party doing the work suffers a reduction in their profits. In many ways, that's completely appropriate though, as the party doing the work and shouldering the risk will also take any extra profit and additional upside if things work out better than expected.

The legal set-up

In addition to the structuring piece we've just discussed, you'll also need to think about the best legal set-up for the joint venture. In general, there are three main options you could consider:

(A) The two JV partners could buy the property in joint names
(B) They could form a company with the JV partners as shareholders
(C) One party buys the property and the other takes a legal charge over it

Under (A), you have the option of a *joint tenancy*, where each of the partners jointly own the property. Alternatively, you could buy as *tenants in common* and agree what proportion of the property each person owns. In (B), where you buy the property through a company, you can specify during the company set up who owns what proportion of the equity, i.e. the ownership structure. Finally, with (C), one party buys the property in their name, but the other party takes a legal charge over the property, providing them with security.

In general, (A) and (B) align more naturally with a profit share structure, and (C) aligns better with a financing agreement structure. However, there are lots of ways to structure the legal set up, and it's impossible to say in advance which one will work best. This will depend on the nature of the project, the parties' tolerance or appetite for different types of risk, and their tax positions. Ideally, you should get input from a tax accountant and a solicitor in helping you decide and set up the legal structures needed.

Keys to success

What we've discussed so far will help you get to the right structure and legal set-up for your joint venture, but there are some other keys to success.

Finding the right partner

Finding and choosing the right partner is as important as finding the right project. It's usually easiest, but not necessarily right, to partner with someone you have an existing relationship with and where there's a good level of trust and respect. This could, for example, be a family member or a close friend; better still would probably be another property professional you know really well. You could also try some active networking at property events to build up the relationships you'll need in advance of when you need them.

When you're broaching the topic of a JV with a potential partner, it's usually best to keep things fairly casual at first and see if they're open to the general idea. If you're the party looking for funds, you should be looking to build credibility by talking about past projects you've worked on. When the time comes, you might also need to sell the specific project you're putting forward as the candidate for your next flip, or at least the type of project you have in mind. If you're the party looking for projects and you have spare cash to invest, then you might need to be the one to make the first move to get the ball rolling. Ultimately, finding and courting a JV partner has more in common with starting a romantic relationship than it does a business transaction. Make sure you approach it this way.

Be clear about your motives

Joint ventures tend to work best when all parties are clear on what each person is bringing to the table and what they're looking to get out. This might sound obvious, but the details are usually less so. For example, in addition to agreement on headline financials and legal set-up, you need to set clear expectations around the level of involvement of both parties, who will be responsible for each aspect of delivery, and who's making what decisions. The day-to-day aspects of how the project will run are as important as the big ticket items you're likely to focus on at the start, and it goes without saying that if a situation crops up that you haven't discussed, you'll likely to be better off dealing with it as a team.

Carry out a pre-mortem

You should try to discuss everything that could go wrong in advance. This is much more difficult to talk about than how you'll spend the profits, but it's important to do this in advance of starting out. You should set aside time specifically for this task. Try to envisage every way the project could go wrong and brainstorm how you would solve each problem. To help with this, you can look at each number in your calculations and think about what might reasonably happen in a worst-case scenario and what you might be able do about it. Think about the lowest price you'd accept for the property, what action you'd take if the project is delayed, e.g. if the property is taking a while to sell or the development works overrun, and what you'll do if the project moves into loss-making territory. Think about your back-up plan if the wider property market falls and you can't sell at all.

Put everything down in writing

Once you're clear on how the JV will work in all the fine detail, you should hire a solicitor to help you put some kind of written agreement together. The document should outline all the important aspects of the deal that each party has committed to, including who is going to do what, the profit share each party will get or the rate of interest agreed, and give sufficient detail on the legal vehicle or security structure that will be used to support the whole transaction.

Ideally, you'll want to work with a solicitor that's used to helping their clients structure this kind of deal, then you can benefit from their experience. Don't be tempted to skip this step. When everything goes well, the written agreement often seems superfluous after the project is complete. But it's when things go wrong on a project that having some kind of agreement in writing comes into its own. Please don't skip this step.

Reversal

Although joint ventures have a lot to offer the aspiring investor, there are times when its best to stay clear altogether. Here are just a few of the situations where JVs might not be the best way forward.

- If it's your first ever flip – If you're the party asking for financial backing, it's not wise to do a joint venture as your first flip. Your reputation is at stake, so you should aim to build up your experience on a project by yourself first.
- The Venn diagram doesn't make sense – If both parties are lacking the same thing, e.g. a particular skillset or experience, and if that thing is essential to executing the project, don't form a joint venture to compensate for this.
- If you don't need to share – In school we're taught that "sharing's caring", but that doesn't need to apply to property. If you have the skills, resources and expertise to pull off the project, why share the gains?

There are plenty of other times too where going it alone is the right option. Make sure to be honest and challenge yourself to get to the right answer for all parties involved. If you're using the joint venture to compensate for a lack of experience, think about other ways you could build up that experience, whether it be by shadowing a fellow investor on a live project or otherwise. If you're looking at joint ventures because of a lack of funds, think about all the ways we discussed in this book to build up your funds faster. There are lots of different ways to succeed in property over the long term, and joint ventures are only one of the ways to win. If you do decide to go down this route, make sure it's right for you.

Play # 27 – Pool your deposits (JV strategy # 2)

Spencer and Patrice had become great friends at university. As biochemistry students, they'd been paired as lab partners, and they'd hit it off from day-one, sharing the same dry sense of humour and love of martial arts movies. Now, in their thirties, they both had plans to invest in property, something they'd discovered at a late-night drinking session in an old haunt, but they each had only £10,000 to invest. Could a joint venture be the answer?

Investing with others

If building up that next deposit is slow, and if you're keen to get some kind of snowball rolling at any cost, then you might consider investing in buy-to-lets with others. The idea is simple – pool your deposits and purchase a buy-to-let property together – but the execution of this strategy still needs careful consideration. This play does for the basic buy-to-let what our last play did for the property flip. It's the second of our joint venture strategies, and its perfect for new investors or for anyone who's suddenly had a drop off in their monthly savings but who's keen to keep the ball rolling.

Keys to success

What makes this joint venture fundamentally different from the last strategy we looked at is the time horizon. With our last play, partner up for a flip, there's a short and definite time horizon for the project; this is usually no longer than a year, if you include the time taken to find, refurbish and sell the property. But with play # 27, pool your deposits, we're considering a longer-term partnership, perhaps five to ten years or more, that is, a suitable time horizon for a typical buy-to-let investment. With that comes a different mindset and a different set of considerations. Let's look at some of the keys to success.

Finding the right partner

This kind of joint venture is less about finding those with complimentary skillsets to work with on a hit-and-run, one-off project and more about building a business (albeit a small one) with a long-term partner. You need to choose a partner with a similar mindset to you and who's looking to invest in property for the same reasons. If you're both looking to generate income, then great; if you're both looking to build wealth through capital growth, then you're on to a winner. But if you want fundamentally different things from the investment, then it's just not going to work. Someone will end up compromising somewhere.

It's worth stressing that the long-term nature of the venture means that this play tends to work best with someone you're planning on staying connected with over the long term – for example, a family member, a spouse, or a lifelong friend. You should also try to keep the number of people involved to a minimum. Two or three people can work okay, but any more tends to get unruly and the different opinions pulling in different directions will eventually lead to a break-up. Think Muse, not the Beatles, Oasis, or Guns n Roses. Even Simon and Garfunkel had an on-off relationship. Make sure you get the personalities right.

Setting up the venture

Of the structuring options we looked at in our last play, the one that makes the most sense for a long-term venture is the profit share. Again, you can vary the profit split, say 60:40 or 70:30, depending what resources each party is bringing to the arrangement. However, from my experience, these things tend to work best when they're kept simple. That is, a 50:50 split for a partnership or a three-way split for a three-party venture. Over time, any differences in the equity split, even a small one, can grate and erode the goodwill that was there at the start.

In terms of the best legal structure for the joint venture, this will depend on a number of factors, including the number of parties involved, their tax positions, and how many properties you're planning to buy together. If the parties are lower rate taxpayers (even after the additional profits are taken into account) and if you're only planning to buy one or two properties, then you'll likely be better off buying in personal names. The additional costs of running a limited company, e.g, accounting and tax compliance, as well as the higher buy-to-let mortgage rates, will likely rule out the company route for most joint ventures.

Ongoing management

When it comes to the ongoing management of the properties, agreeing who does what is important. You should try to set out in writing how you'll handle each component of the day-to-day management, from advertising and letting out the property to repairs and maintenance. Even if you're planning to outsource all of this to a letting agent, you'll still need to agree how you'll make any decisions on things like what level of rent to charge, whether to furnish the property, and the standard of any repairs. You should also agree how you'll resolve conflicts.

If at all possible, you should try to set up a shared business bank account for the joint venture. This will be a necessity if you're establishing the JV through a limited company, but you should also try to do this if you purchase the property in your personal names. That way, each party has visibility on what's going on with the property day-to-day, including the cash flow generated and what costs are being incurred. Make sure your letting agent provides a copy of their monthly statements to all JV partners as well.

Taking profits (or supporting losses) and exit strategy

It might sound crazy, but one of the biggest tensions that can arise in this type of joint venture is what to do with the profits. You've made some money, but should you take it all out, hold some back as a buffer against future adverse experience, or even use it to buy additional properties. You should get clear on this right from the start and agree a profit management plan between all the JV partners. This is even more important if things go wrong and the parties need to inject additional funds to support a loss-making venture. Usually this will manifest as a question around who will pay for some large, one-off cost or another, something you don't want to be deciding after the fact.

Finally, you'll also need to agree an approach to ending the joint venture. This could mean deciding on what conditions you intend to sell the property or what to do if you have different opinions. For example, you could agree to sell the property if it experiences a large capital gain of a defined order of magnitude or if the property has been loss-making or cashflow negative for a number of years. You could also agree that if you disagree on the future of the investment, i.e. if one party wants to keep the property and the other wants to sell, then the party who wants to keep it will endeavour to buy the other party out within an agreed time period, say one to two years. If that's not possible, then the only option may be to sell up and part ways on the joint venture.

Reversal

There are many investors out there who will say it's not a good idea to enter into a long-term joint venture of this nature. The reasons commonly cited are that it's complicated, people's needs and expectations change over time, and that it can lead to disagreements on how the investment should be run. However, long term JVs happen all the time in business – be it a manufacturer looking for access to an overseas market, a service provider partnering with a technology start-up, or a franchisor partnering with a franchisee – and there's no reason they can't work in property, provided you go about it the right way and enter into the agreement in good faith. The only time I would seriously advise against a long-term JV of this nature is if you envisage needing to pull your monies out after only a short period of time, in which case buy-to-let is probably not the right property strategy for you in the first place.

Redux

Taken to the extreme, i.e. when you have multiple JV partners, this play is nothing more than a form of crowdfunding. So, rather than creating your own property JV from scratch, you could consider investing through one of the crowdfunding property websites already out there.

The kind of platforms that exist right now allow you to pick an investment property on their website and choose how much you'd like to invest. Your money is then pooled with that of other investors to buy the property, and you simply get paid a share of the rental income and any gains when the property is sold. The investment vehicle is commonly a special purpose vehicle (or SPV) that's created to own the property and the investors own shares in the SPV. The crowdfunding platform then makes all the decisions around the day-to-day management of the property, so it can be a relatively hands-off investment.

With a minimum investment threshold of £5,000, these platforms offer a way of getting started in property sooner than you otherwise might, which is a major advantage. They also offer investors with smaller amounts of money to invest a way to diversify their portfolio, but there are potential downsides. The main one for me is the lack of track record. Because many of these platforms are relatively new, it's difficult to know which one is the best and which ones are trustworthy. For me, that makes it a relatively risky proposition at the present time, though this could change in the future. The other downsides here are the loss of control, the lower returns you can expect after the platform has taken its cut, and the lack of liquidity or secondary market to sell your stake in the property.

Crowd funding platforms of this nature offer a kind of half-way house between direct property investment and residential and commercial property funds, which are more diversified, your money being pooled with thousands of other investors. If you want to get started in property sooner and you're not comfortable with the risks that arise from either JVs or crowdfunding platforms, then you might be better off waiting until your savings have grown to the size where you can go-it-alone or invest in an established residential or commercial property fund. They still have the same downsides, i.e. loss of control and investment fees, but they have the upside of being more established and have a liquid secondary market should you choose to exit.

Play # 28 – Short term / holiday lets (aka the airbnb strategy)

Ever since he sold his graphic design agency two years ago, Michael had been looking for a way to get into property. He lived in a lovely seaside town in Cornwall, along with his wife Maggie and their children. He wanted to invest locally and manage the properties himself, seeing himself more of a landlord than an investor, but the high property prices in the area made the yields on regular buy-to-let investments unattractive. He wondered whether a holiday let business might be a profitable alternative. Because he'd run a successful business himself for over ten years, he was certain that he and Maggie could run this successfully. They would need some help marketing the property, but being based locally they could take care of the cleaning, the changeovers and the check-ins themselves, which would help bring down their costs.

A change of scenery

With staycations rising in popularity amongst British holidaymakers, so too has the popularity of the holiday let as an investment proposition. In our next play, we're going to look at some of the pros and cons of this type of investment, we'll put together a worked example to show you how you might approach the figures, and we'll discuss how to run a successful holiday let. Don't be seduced by the prospect of three weeks in the Lake District during the off-season, this type of investment needs to be run like a business if it's going to succeed, and there's lots of work involved compared with the basic buy-to-let investment. A permanent vacation it most certainly is not. Like any business in the hospitality sector, you are there to serve others, and your needs should come second to those of the business. If you're still interested, then carry on reading.

The pros and cons

The holiday let is a completely different beast to a regular buy-to-let. It has more in common with running a hotel or travel business than it does with running a property rental business. That being said, there is some crossover in the skills needed, particularly around things like finding and building the investment case, financing the deal, and building the systems and processes needed to run the business smoothly. Let's look at the pros and cons of this kind of investment.

What are the positives?

- You can make more money – If you buy in the right location and you get the marketing, ongoing management, and changeovers right, then it can be more profitable than a regular buy-to-let – otherwise why do it in the first place? As a rule of thumb, you could potentially make up to 50% more than a regular buy-to-let investment, after all the extra costs have been factored in.
- Hacking the yield – There are parts of the UK where the yields are too low for buy-to-let to makes sense. At the time of writing, this would include much of London and the South East of England. In these locations, short term lets offer investors a way to "hack" the yield and give them a way to invest in areas that wouldn't make sense otherwise.
- Spreading the tenant risk – With a regular buy-to-let, there's always a chance you could end up with a problem tenant. With holiday lets, you're spreading this risk, as a bad tenant will potentially only stay for a week or two at the most. In addition, the general level of wear and tear tends to be lower.
- You get to stay there – Yes, I know I said that the needs of the business should come first, but one of the positives of owning a holiday let is that you might

get to use the property yourself at certain times of the year. You shouldn't be using it yourself during the peak summer months, but there's no reason why you can't grab a week or two there yourself in the off-season.

What are the negatives?

- Higher set-up costs – Holiday lets need to be furnished to a higher standard. You'll need to provide everything that the holidaymaker might reasonably need at the property, down to the last item of cooking equipment, crockery, and a corkscrew for that bottle of red. Because of this, the set-up costs tend to be higher than for a regular buy-to-let.
- The income is uncertain – There is a potential for higher revenue, but the income generated by a holiday let also tends to be more uncertain. The level of occupancy achieved and the average weekly rent are difficult to predict in advance and can vary from one year to the next. If you get your assumptions wrong, you could end up in a loss-making position more easily.
- It takes a lot more work – There's a lot more work involved than a regular buy-to-let investment, including the marketing, day-to-day management and the changeovers. Even if you decide to outsource this to a letting agent, you'll need to stay close to how they're running it – there are less management companies available for holiday lets, so finding a good one is harder.
- Running costs are higher – The costs of running a holiday let are substantially higher than a traditional buy-to-let. You'll need to pay higher management fees and higher mortgage costs, cover the cost of utilities and subscriptions, and pay for cleaning and laundry at each changeover. This is all in addition to the costs you would incur with a regular buy-to-let investment.

A worked example

To understand how the figures work for a holiday let, it's useful to take a look at a worked example. I've linked in with a friend of mine on this for an example, as she does more of these types of deals than I do. The example below is for a two-bedroom, one-bathroom apartment in Bath city centre, within half a mile of the main train station. She picked this location because of its attractiveness as a holiday hotspot and because Bath is also a vibrant city in its own right, giving her the back-up option of running this as a regular buy-to-let, if things don't work out as planned.

She approached the research like you would a regular buy-to-let investment. She used Rightmove to estimate the market value of the property and she used a number of holiday booking sites, mainly airbnb and www.holidaylettings.co.uk, to get a feeling for the average price per night the property could rent for in the peak season, the shoulder months, and in the off-season. The key assumptions in the modelling are as follows: (a) that we can secure the property for £300,000, a little bit under the asking, but not unachievable; (b) we purchase the property with a 70% loan-to-value interest only mortgage with a 2.5% p.a. interest rate; (c) that we will use a letting agent to manage the property for us, who will take care of marketing, day-to-day management, and coordination of the handovers; (d) the cash we invest is £110,000, that is, £90,000 for the deposit, calculated as 30% × £300,000, plus £14,000 for stamp duty and £6,000 to cover legal expenses and the cost of setting up the property up as a holiday let.

There are a lot of different numbers in the table below, so I'm going to break down the figures step-by-step, looking at the assumptions we've made and how each of the figures has been calculated. You'll then be able to adapt this example, if you try to model a holiday let for yourself in the future, but please do make sure you revise all the figures based on your own research and expectations.

Projected revenues

In the example below, we've assumed we'll be able to rent out the property for £150 per night in peak season. We've assumed there are 10 weeks per year in peak season, six weeks in summer and two weeks at Christmas and Easter and that these weeks would be fully occupied. This gives a projected revenue of £150 × 7 nights × 10 weeks equals £10,500 under each of the scenarios.

Occupancy level	Low	Medium	High
Number of weeks occupied	24 weeks	30 weeks	36 weeks
Occupancy rate	46%	58%	69%
Number of changeovers	24	30	36

Projected revenues

	Low	Medium	High
Peak season	£10,500	£10,500	£10,500
Shoulder months	£8,400	£8,400	£8,400
Off-season	£2,520	£6,300	£10,080
Total revenue	£21,420	£25,200	£28,980

Projected costs

	Low	Medium	High
Service charge & ground rent	£1,250	£1,250	£1,250
Utilities and subscriptions	£2,100	£2,100	£2,100
Management fees (Revenue × 24%)	£5,141	£6,048	£6,955
Repairs	£500	£500	£500
Insurance	£300	£300	£300
Wear and tear	£1,000	£1,000	£1,000
Mortgage costs	£5,250	£5,250	£5,250
Compliance and safety checks	£200	£200	£200
Changeover costs, e.g. cleaning	£2,040	£2,550	£3,060
Total costs	£17,781	£19,198	£20,615

	Low	Medium	High
Annual profit	£3,639	£6,002	£8,365
Average cash flow per month	£303	£500	£697

	Low	Medium	High
Cash invested	£110,000	£110,000	£110,000
Estimated ROI	3.3% p.a.	5.5% p.a.	7.6% p.a.

In the shoulder months, we've assumed 10 weeks of occupancy at a medium nightly rate of £120 and again we've assumed these would be fully occupied. This gives a projected revenue of £120 × 7 nights × 10 weeks equals £8,400 across all the scenarios. Lastly, we've made the assumption that in the off-season we would achieve a nightly rate of £90 and that we would achieve occupancy of 4 additional weeks in the low scenario, 10 additional weeks in the medium scenario, and 16 additional weeks in the high occupancy scenario. This gives projected off-season revenue of £2,520 for the low occupancy scenario, £6,300 for the medium case, and £10,080 for the high occupancy scenario.

These scenarios represent a total occupancy of 24, 30 and 36 weeks across the whole year, that is, occupancy rates of 46%, 58% and 69% respectively. It's worth noting that the average occupancy level for a typical UK holiday let in a strong location is around 60% per year, close to our medium scenario.

Management fees and changeover costs

Management fees tend to be higher than for traditional buy-to-let investments, as there's more work involved in marketing and managing the property. The average management fee for a holiday let is around 20% plus VAT, i.e. a total of 24% of revenues. In the example above, we've calculated the management fee as 24% of revenues for each of the scenarios.

At changeovers, the holiday let will need to be cleaned and the linen will need to be changed. We've assumed a cost per changeover of £85, which breaks down as £50 for the cleaning, £25 for fresh linen, and £10 for a welcome basket. We've also assumed that guests stay seven nights on average, meaning there will be 24, 30 and 36 changeovers needed under the low, medium and high occupancy scenarios respectively. Together, the management fee and the changeover costs are the largest extra costs compared with a traditional buy-to-let.

Other costs

With a holiday let, you'll need to cover all the utility costs, relating to things like electricity, heating, water and potentially refuse collection, as your business will be classified as a self-catering business. You'll likely also need to cover the cost of a phone line, broadband, TV licence and any subscriptions you want your guests to be able to access, e.g. Netflix or Amazon. We've assumed £175 per month or £2,100 per year to cover these costs.

We've also included a range of other costs in the modelling. The service charge and ground rent of £1,250 was based on last year's cost, which we obtained from the estate agent. We've allowed £500 for maintenance and repairs, which is not unreasonable for an apartment, and £1,000 for wear and tear, e.g. redecoration and replacement of furniture from time-to-time. We've added £300 for insurance, including public liability insurance, £200 for any compliance and safety checks needed, e.g. gas safety, electrical testing, etc. And we've modelled the cost of our interest only mortgage based on a 2.5% p.a. rate, i.e. a £210,000 loan amount × 2.5% equals £5,250 per year.

What does this tell us?

The results of our modelling above show us that this two-bedroom apartment could potentially work as a holiday let. The ROI we obtain is going to be highly dependent on the final occupancy rate we achieve, with a 3.3% p.a. ROI in the case where we achieve a low occupancy of 46% and a 5.5% p.a. ROI in the case where we achieve a medium occupancy of 58%, just below the industry average. We might even be able to obtain an ROI of up to 7.6% p.a. if we achieve a high occupancy of 69%. So, how does this compare with a buy-to-let property in the same area of Bath?

Well, we ran the numbers for the same property, but assuming you used it as a traditional buy-to-let instead. Using a monthly rent of £1,200 in the calculation, this gave us an expected ROI of 4.0% p.a. for the same property, using a 70% loan-to-value mortgage for consistency. So, the yield on the holiday let is higher than the buy-to-let yield in the medium and high occupancy scenarios, but you have to work a lot harder to achieve this yield. Also, with the holiday let, there's a much greater chance you could end up in a loss-making position, if your assumptions around occupancy and nightly rates turn out to be wrong.

How to run a successful holiday let

Now that we've looked at a worked example and we have a better feel for the pros and cons of this type of investment, let's turn our attention to the things you can do to run a holiday let successfully. Here are my seven top tips.

1. Pick the right location – If you pick the right location, everything else will be a lot easier. Stick to tried-and-tested holiday destinations with strong rental demand and strong transport links. If you're hedging your bets, try not to go too rural, as this will make it more difficult to execute a back-up plan like using the property as a regular buy-to-let if things go wrong. Ultimately, you need to research the area thoroughly and be led by the investment case.

2. Maximising the occupancy rate – As we saw above, your final profit and the ROI you achieve will depend heavily on the level of occupancy. With the right marketing and pricing, you should find it straightforward to fill the property in the peak and shoulder months, but you'll need to work harder to fill it in the off-season. This is what will turn your ROI from average to great.

3. Getting the marketing right – If you're marketing the property yourself, you need to take great photos and write a great advert. You can advertise your property on sites like airbnb or www.holidaylettings.co.uk. As a longer-term strategy, you could try to build your own website and get it ranked in Google – this is a hard route to take, but it can be worth it if you get it right. You might also be able to use social media. If you've outsourced this to an agent, check in with them regularly and input where needed to move this along.

4. Provide great customer service – They're spending a decent chunk of their hard-earned cash, so holidaymakers expect great customer service. You need to respond quickly to guests' enquires before, during, and after their stay and deal professionally with bookings and payments. If you've outsourced the management, you need to find an agent who will do this for you. To help with this, I recommend writing a holiday let manual, which gives full details about

the property and what you will and won't accept to the agent, so they don't need to bother you with every last question from a potential guest.

5. Think like an accountant – Here's a quick question for you – is it worth you accepting a booking for one night only? The answer is probably not. If your extra revenue from a single night is £90, but you will pay £22 of this to your management company and £85 for the changeover costs, then you'll make a loss of £17 if you accept this booking. Make sure your managing agent knows if you have a minimum number of nights rule. Platforms like airbnb let you add a cleaning fee to the overall booking cost to help you to manage this issue.

6. Understand the tax rules – Holiday lets are taxed differently than traditional buy-to-lets, so speak to an accountant to make sure you know the latest rules. They are treated differently from a VAT perspective, meaning you may need to become VAT registered if you have a large portfolio of holiday lets. In addition, there are differences in the way mortgage interest costs are treated for tax purposes, if you buy in your personal name.

7. Register for business rates – Finally, if your property is available to let for 20 weeks or more per year, then it will be rated as self-catering property and it needs to be valued for business rates. This means you'll need to pay business rates, instead of council tax. However, if the "rateable value" of the property, which you'll discuss with HMRC's valuation office, is less than £12,000, then you may be eligible for small business rate relief and pay no business rates.

Common pitfalls and mistakes

The main pitfalls and mistakes that can arise with this strategy are when people treat the whole venture a bit too casually. Here are some common ones:

- Not checking the terms of the lease – If you're buying a leasehold property, then you need to check the terms of the lease before you buy. Many leases prohibit subletting the property on a short-term basis, e.g. less than three months, which means you wouldn't be able to use it as a holiday let.

- Not getting a specialist mortgage – You need to make sure that you take out the right mortgage product, which means you'll need a mortgage specifically for holiday lets. The interest rates on these products tend to be higher and the choice is also more restricted. Check all the details, as some mortgages specifically for holiday lets don't allow the use of airbnb platforms.
- Falling down on compliance – You need to make sure that you're complying with all the necessary rules and regulations around holiday lets, whether that be health and safety, local laws and restrictions, and tax rules. If you're new to holiday lets, make sure you research these thoroughly.

As a final word of caution, you need to know what you're getting into with this type of property venture. You're running a hospitality business, and it's not something you should take on unless you're up for the extra work involved and you think you'll enjoy it. If you're more of a "set it and forget it" type of property investor with little time on your hands, this strategy might not be for you.

Play # 29 – Run your property as serviced accommodation

Sophia owned a range of properties, everything from three-bedroom family buy-to-lets in commuter towns to one and two-bedroom apartments in city centres. At a networking event, she'd chatted with someone who'd turned their city centre properties into serviced accommodation, and she wondered if that was a strategy that might suit her. What she couldn't work out from the conversation was whether this strategy was just another flash in the pan, the latest property fad if you will, or whether it was a strategy that had legs. She wondered what it was all about, how to get started with something like this, and what it would take to succeed. She had some research to do.

What is serviced accommodation?

Serviced accommodation is a growing trend in the UK property market. The term is an umbrella term for furnished accommodation that's available for both short term and long term let. As a strategy, it's different from holiday lets, which we looked at in out last play, as it tends to be targeted at the corporate rental market. At the same time, however, it's also different from buy-to-lets, where tenants rent out properties on long-term AST agreements of between six and twelve months. Serviced accommodation is a strategy that plays in the middle, somewhere in between short term lets and long term buy-to-lets, and it shares features with both of these strategies.

Properties aimed at serviced accommodation are furnished apartments in city centres or locations with strong transport links. They're usually available to let anywhere from a couple of weeks to three months or more, and the tenant profile tends to be more corporate focussed. For example, tenants might be contractors moving around for work, employees on secondment, or corporate executives on a relocation programme. From a corporate perspective, serviced accommodation is cheaper than hotels and it offers a more normal way of life, as guests can cook for themselves, watch TV, and even do some laundry. With all of that in mind, let's look at some of the pros and cons of this kind of property strategy.

The pros and cons

What are the positives?

- Higher nightly rates – If you buy in the right location, the average nightly rate you receive from serviced accommodation will be higher than a regular buy-to-let. For short stays of one-to-two weeks, this will be similar to holiday lets; for stays of one to three months, the rate will be lower than for a holiday let, but still higher than a buy-to-let.

- High occupancy levels – The average reported occupancy level for serviced accommodation in the UK is around 80%. Some properties will even achieve occupancy close to 90%. Good managing agents will look to fill in the voids between those one and three-month corporate tenancies with short-stay guests, potentially even holidaymakers, if there's demand in the area. Overall, the occupancy level achieved should be higher than a holiday let.

- A better tenant profile – In general, short-stay guests take better care of your property. The property itself will likely be getting a weekly clean, so it's going to be kept in great condition all year round; what's more, there will be lots of opportunity to attend to smaller repairs and fixes in between guest stays, while the property is vacant. In short, you can expect better tenants and less damage with a serviced accommodation strategy.

What are the negatives?

- Higher set-up costs – Like holiday lets, serviced accommodation units need to be furnished to a higher standard. You'll need to provide everything guests might need, including cooking facilities and equipment, entertainment like a TV and Wi-Fi, and appliances like dishwashers and washing machines. As such, the set-up costs tend to be higher than a regular buy-to-let.

- It takes a lot more work – There's a lot more work involved than traditional buy-to-let investment, including the marketing, day-to-day management and the changeovers. If you decide to outsource this to a management company, which is a good idea if you're not an expert in this area yourself, you'll need to stay close to how they run it day-to-day.

- Running costs are higher – The running costs for serviced accommodation tend to be higher than buy-to-lets, but lower than holiday lets. You'll need to pay higher management fees and higher mortgage costs, cover the cost of all utilities and subscriptions, and pay for cleaning and fresh linen each week. However, the volume of changeovers is usually lower than for holiday lets.

What kind of facilities to offer?

If you decide to go the serviced accommodation route, you'll need to make some decisions about what services you want to offer. In general, serviced apartments tend to offer guests most of the following:

- cooking facilities and a fully equipped kitchen
- a washing machine for guests to do their own laundry
- one to two bedrooms and a bathroom or ensuite
- a separate living area with a TV and internet access
- a weekly housekeeping service, including cleaning and fresh linen
- all utilities, i.e. water, heating, and electricity, included

The properties themselves will often be located in residential buildings that may or may not have on-site staff. Buildings with access to other "hotel-like" services, e.g. residents' gyms, on-site meeting rooms, or a concierge service, can work well. Although these types of properties tend to attract higher service charges, these extras services are highly sought after, and they can make the difference between a potential client choosing your property over another similar property nearby. A 24-hour concierge or helpdesk is extremely useful, if it can be used as a place to store keys and facilitate check-ins and check-outs. Be careful with this, as not all concierge services are permitted to hold keys.

Keys to success

Now that we've thought about some of the services we might offer and we have a better feel for the pros and cons, let's turn our attention to some of the keys to success with serviced accommodation. Here are my top five tips.

1. Pick the right location – The kinds of locations that tend to work best for this strategy are city centres and areas with strong transport links. This strategy is focussed on corporate tenants, so you'll want to buy in cities that are strong employment centres and which house a lot of corporate HQs, ensuring there is ongoing demand from secondees and the corporate relocation market.

2. Pick the right property – Small houses can work well in certain locations, but in general this strategy works best with one and two-bedroom apartments. So, there is some crossover with the kinds of properties you might think about buying as regular buy-to-let investments. Studios tend to be too small; three-bedroom flats are a bit too big and could inadvertently create a HMO.

3. Get your modelling right – I haven't provided a worked example, but you can approach the modelling the same way you would for a holiday let. You need to work out your average nightly rate and your expected occupancy level. Make sure your assumptions are prudent; if you're new to a particular city, speak to some local managing agents about the kinds of average nightly rates

and occupancy levels you could achieve in the area. Make sure you factor in all costs, including that weekly cleaning cost. Fees for managing agents tend to be around 15% plus VAT (around 18% gross) of your revenue.

4. Choose a specialist letting agent – Your average, high-street letting agent is unlikely to have the connections and experience needed to run your property as serviced accommodation. As such, you'll need to choose a specialist letting agent that has good links to the corporate market and a strong track record in this particular sector. Choosing the right partner is likely to be the single most important factor for success with this strategy, so don't overlook this. And unless you have a strong network yourself, don't go this one alone.

5. Choosing the right commission structure – Managing agents in the serviced accommodation sector offer a range of fee structures to their clients. I would stay clear of fee structures offering a "guaranteed rental income" where the agents will pay you a fixed return each month, as the agent will want to keep any upside they achieve. Try to stick with a simple fee structure like 15% plus VAT of rental income generated and make sure you scour the contract for any extra fees or charges they might want to add on.

Finally, it's worth saying that you'll want your management company to pick up all queries from guests. As with a holiday let, you can draft a house manual you leave with the agent to answer common queries. You can also leave a laminated copy of the manual at the property, so new guests have instructions on how to operate the appliances – that way, you won't get questions and phone calls from guests at 2 am asking how the heating works.

Common pitfalls and mistakes

Because serviced accommodation is a relatively new idea to most UK property investors, it can be difficult to find good educational materials. This is particularly true about the potential pitfalls and mistakes, as most of the materials out there and online are trying to sell the concept. Here are some common ones:

- Not checking the terms of the lease – If you're buying a leasehold property, then you need to check the terms of the lease before you buy. Many leases prohibit subletting the property on a short-term basis, e.g. less than three months, which means you wouldn't be able to use it in this way.

- Not getting a specialist mortgage – You need to make sure you take out the right mortgage product, which means you'll need a commercial mortgage specifically for this strategy. The interest rates on these products tend to be higher and the choice is also more restricted. Check all the details, as some mortgages still don't allow the use of airbnb platforms.

- Falling down on compliance – You need to make sure you're complying with all the necessary rules and regulations around serviced accommodation, be it health and safety laws, any local rules restrictions, and tax rules. If you're new to this strategy, research it thoroughly before you start out.

- Trying to go it alone – I touched on this above, but serviced accommodation is a strategy that is difficult to execute by yourself, as you're unlikely to have strong links with the corporate lettings market, which is what this play is all about. If you go it alone and try to do all the marketing yourself on platforms like airbnb and booking.com, you'll just end up running a holiday let.

As a final tip, it's worth getting clear upfront with your managing agent on the kinds of tenants you will and won't accept. If you don't accept smokers, children, under 21s, or pets, then you need to let them know. Also, you'll want to set a minimum number of nights, as we saw for the holiday let play, otherwise you risk servicing a guest and making a loss. For example, if you said no bookings shorter than one week, this might be a good rule for serviced accommodation, as it will encourage your agent to stick to the core strategy of servicing corporate clients.

Play # 30 – Sweating your property assets

Nadia's first two buy-to-let investments worked out well. When she looked back at the ROI she was achieving a couple of years in, the returns were bang on what she'd expected in her pre-deal modelling. For a time, she thought this was testament to her robust due diligence and prudent nature, but when her third and fourth buy-to-let deals started to underperform, her halo slipped. She needed a way to sweat her properties harder and squeeze more juice from them to meet her return targets and get her long-term property goals back-on-track. There was a lot to consider and many things she could try, but were there any obvious quick wins?

Now that you own some assets

Up to this point, we've mainly focussed on how to build a capital base and how to acquire property assets. Over the long term, it's equally important to understand how to run a property rental business day-to-day and how to maximise your profits. These profits can be reinvested to grow your portfolio and will compound over time through the snowball effect, so what might seem like an incremental improvement can actually be much more.

This play is all about sweating your property assets. We're going to look at how you can improve the performance of your investments at a granular level – that is, we're going to run through each of the different areas that contribute to the overall performance, and we're going to discuss what levers you can pull to increase your investment returns. We're mainly going to consider simple buy-to-let properties here, but you can apply these same principles and ideas to any type of rental unit in your portfolio. Whether you're an experienced investor or a new investor looking to make their mark, I'm confident you'll find something in here to improve what you're doing each and every day.

Increasing your income

Like any other business, the profit you make is the difference between the income you receive and the expenses you incur. To start with, we're going to take a look at how to improve the income you generate from a rental property.

Maximising your potential rental income

The *market rental income* is the maximum amount of rent the property could theoretically collect. In an ideal world, you would charge 100% of the market rent for your property all the time. However, this doesn't always happen in practice, for a variety of reasons. Our aim when we're letting out our property should be to get as close to this theoretical maximum as we can.

To estimate the market rental income, we need to conduct a survey of the market. This is a simple process and you should do this at least annually. You can do a search on Rightmove or your favourite portal to see what similar properties are being marketed for right now. The closer the comparables you use, the better your estimate. You can also "shop" your properties by calling some local letting agents to ask them what the property could let for in the current market.

Your *potential rental income* on the other hand is the income your property would generate at the current agreed rent assuming the property is 100% occupied all year round with no voids and missed rental payments. Maximising your potential rental income is fairly straightforward. You should review the rents you charge regularly, usually at the end of a tenancy, to make sure they're tracking rents in the local area. Before you market the property, speak to your letting agent and get comfortable with their proposed level of rent. There are also a number of practical things you can do to make sure your property is viewed at its best. This will enhance your chances of securing top dollar and maximising your potential rental income.

- Advertise early – Advertise before the existing tenancy comes to an end to increase the number of new tenant leads generated.
- Cleaning and repairs – Get the property cleaned and attend to any repairs on day one of the void to ensure your property is viewed at its best.
- Take great photos and run a great advert – You want to attract a lot of interest and drum up multiple interest parties that will compete with each other.
- Viewings – Consider the time of day the property looks at its best and conduct viewings then. Open up the windows, make sure it smells great.
- Negotiate – For example, if the tenant wants extra storage, you could agree to provide this, as long as they agree to pay the full rental price.
- Furnishings – If you decide to let out your property as a furnished let, make sure any furniture you provide is good quality and fit-for-purpose.

If you're going to use a letting agent, make sure they are doing all these things on your behalf. If you're investing from afar, you'll likely have to make a few calls to your letting agent and make sure your property gets the attention it deserves. Don't feel bad about this, just stay polite and be persistent.

Reducing voids and other losses

So, we've looked at how to maximise your potential rental income. The flip side of the coin is the amount of lost rental income from voids and other losses. In order to increase your income, you'll want to minimise any void periods, i.e. the number of days the property is sitting empty. You'll also want to minimise any other losses, e.g. missed rental payments or losses incurred where the deposit was insufficient to cover the damage left by the tenant.

Every investor will have their own tolerance level for void periods, based on their modelling when they bought the property. Generally, I aim to keep the lost rental income from voids to below 5% of the potential rental income, averaged over several years. In practice, this means that I need to keep voids to less than two weeks if my tenant changes every year. If my tenant stays for two years on average, then I'll have more like one month to turn around the property.

There are two general strategies you can employ to reduce voids. The first is to encourage the tenant to stay for longer. A competitively priced rent will help with this, as will taking care of your tenants and responding to requests promptly. Letting a property unfurnished can also help with this, as the effort put into furnishing a property by the tenant creates a barrier to them leaving. The second strategy is to do everything you can to turn the property around quickly. The single biggest thing you can do here is get your agent to start marketing the property a month or two before the existing tenancy ends and to line up viewings in advance. As discussed above, you should also make sure you attend to any cleaning required or repairs needed as soon as the tenant leaves.

The level of other losses from rental arrears and damage tends to vary from property to property. If you're investing in strong city centre locations and going for professional tenants, you'll be hoping for a low level of losses here. However, depending on the location of the property and the demographic profile of tenants in that area, you might find you do need to budget for some degree of losses here. Decreasing these other losses then is all about your choice of property and your choice of tenant.

Make sure you screen tenants carefully through your reference checks and do not give someone the benefit of the doubt. If they have a bad credit history, you should insist on a guarantor or better still look for an alternative tenant. Where you can, stick with tenants with a strong employment history, meaning both long service with a single employer and some level of professional qualifications in an industry that's in demand. No industry is 100% recession-proof, and you never truly know a tenant until they move in. However, you can certainly try your best to avoid problem tenants from the start.

Other sources of income

This area doesn't get any attention in most property books, but it is possible to make some extra income in addition to the rental income. The type of income you can generate will depend on what's common in the local market, your property management objectives, and the type of business you want to run. You'll also have to adhere to any local laws and regulations around fees you can and can't charge your tenants. The important thing is to treat this as a business and to have a think about how to optimise the income you can generate. Here's a quick list of ideas and some areas where you might be able to generate extra income.

- Parking – Depending on supply and demand, you might be able to charge £50 to £150 per month for parking. On the supply side, you could buy a space, or you could rent one from someone else.
- Pet rent – Pet owners often have a limited choice of accommodation. As such, pet owners are often prepared to pay more rent. You might be able to charge £25 to £50 a month, depending on the pet.
- Cleaning service – You could offer tenants a cleaning service, then arrange for this to be provided by a local cleaner. If the fee you charge is greater than the cost of hiring a cleaner, then you're in-the-money.
- Laundry service – You could offer a laundry service, perhaps a pick up and return dry cleaning service. Again, you could charge a fee, then cut a deal with a local dry cleaner and pocket the difference.
- Moving in and out – There might be opportunities for renting out storage space to tenants on a temporary basis or perhaps supporting tenants with their move. Also, you could think about hiring out furniture to tenants.

These are just a few ideas, but I'm sure there are more you could use to generate extra income. There are lots of opportunities here for creative investors, and if you can generate some level of extra income, it can boost your ROI and turn an average property investment into a great one.

Decreasing your expenses

Generally speaking, running costs are much more controllable than income. For this reason, controlling your expenses is the single most important thing you can do to improve your investment returns. You should pay close attention to your budgeted expenses over the course of the year to make sure these stay on-track. If they go off-track, you should look into why and see what you can do about it. Here are just a few things you can do to control your costs.

- Ground rent and service cost – If you own an apartment or a leasehold house, you'll need to pay service costs and ground rent. In the main, there's little you can do to control these costs, but you can make sure you've budgeted for them prudently before you buy the property.
- Professional fees – The bulk of these costs will be property management fees, including costs in relation to marketing and tenancy renewals. Shop around for the best deal with local letting agents; as your portfolio grows in size, try to strike a bulk discount. You could also self-manage to cut your costs, but you should think about the extra time this will take.
- Premises insurance – This will include the cost of buildings and landlord's insurance. For the policies you arrange yourself, you can call a broker and get competing bids to try to lower the cost. You might also be able to play around with the level of cover and excesses on the policy.
- Repairs and maintenance – These costs will vary depending on the age, type and state of repair of the property. To reduce costs, you can shop around for tradespeople and ask for several quotes. You should also make sure to act on any maintenance requests promptly to prevent unnecessary damage.
- Finance costs – For most investors, finance costs will be one of their biggest expenses. The main lever we can pull to reduce these costs is to shop around for better mortgage deals. At the end of each fixed-rate period, speak to your mortgage broker to see what deals are available on the market.

Setting yourself a budget for each property in your portfolio and monitoring your costs over time is one of the best things you can do to maximise your returns. If your investments are not working out as expected and your ROI is lower than you hoped for when you bought the property, then you'll need to figure out why and what you can do about it.

Further reading and useful resources

Studying your portfolio at the property-by-property level and analysing all the factors that contribute to that performance can be extremely enlightening. It will force you to be objective about the results your achieving, act as a catalyst for any action that's needed, and keep you focussed over the long term. As the old saying goes, what gets measured, gets managed.

If you decide you want to put this analysis on a firmer footing, you should check my first book, *Essential Property Investment Calculations.* In Chapter 7, how to measure property returns, and Chapter 8, property management KPIs, I cover a range of key metrics and calculations you can use to assess the performance of your portfolio at the total portfolio level and on a property-by-property basis. There's also a chapter on portfolio risk management to help you manage the risks involved in running a property portfolio over time.

Conclusion

That brings us to the end of Volume 1 of *The Property Investment Playbook*. You now have an overview of all the common strategies, tactics and key principles that successful investors use to build their property portfolios. You've built up a working knowledge of the most common types of investment that new investors turn to, including the basic buy-to-let, light refurbishments, short-term holiday lets, and serviced accommodation. We've also covered a variety of key financing techniques, one-off ventures you can use to earn chunks of cash for reinvestment, like property flips, and how to use different types of joint venture to build your portfolio with help from others. These strategies and techniques are at the core of what most property investors do, and they're the plays you'll want to master first before moving on to more complex ideas.

With all of that said, there will come a time when you feel ready for a new property challenge, when you want to break the shackles and move on to bigger and better things. That's where Volume 2 comes in. Volume 2 of The Property Investment Playbook is a whole new series of plays, strategies and techniques for the more advanced property investor. It includes plays about how to grow your portfolio, a dedicated section for experienced investors, including ten advanced investment strategies, and a whole host of other property tips and techniques. When you're ready for that, I hope you'll check it out to see if there's something in there that could take your property journey to the next level. In the meantime, I hope you've enjoyed this book and that it's one you'll keep coming back to in the future. Best of luck with your future property endeavours.

Get the free resources

I've prepared some free materials to accompany the book. All you need to do to access them is head over to my website. These materials include the following:

- a "dreamlining" spreadsheet to help you set your property goals
- a spreadsheet for assessing basic buy-to-let property deals
- a spreadsheet for modelling property refurbishments
- a spreadsheet for modelling short term / holiday lets

The spreadsheets are the ones I use personally in my own property investments. It's all completely free with no sell on. Just sign up at my website at:

www.essentialproperty.net/playbook-vol-1

Printed in Great Britain
by Amazon

85669006R00123